THE

BY THE EDITORS OF
AMERICAN HERITAGE
The Magazine of History

AUTHOR
RALPH K. ANDRIST

CONSULTANT
CARTER GOODRICH
Department of Economics, Columbia University

PUBLISHED BY
AMERICAN HERITAGE
PUBLISHING CO., INC.
New York

BOOK TRADE AND INSTITUTIONAL DISTRIBUTION BY
HARPER & ROW

ALBANY INSTITUTE OF HISTORY AND ART

ERIE CANAL

FIRST EDITION

FOREWORD

History abounds with the engineering projects of pharaohs, caesars, and kings, built with the taxes and toil of their unwilling subjects. But the decision to build the 363-mile Erie Canal in 1817 was an answer to the demands of a newly free and democratic people.

A man-made waterway, spanning valleys and rivers, channeling through hills of solid rock or climbing over them, flowing across marshes and thickly-wooded forests, all the way across New York State—it seemed to be a preposterous idea. Even President Jefferson, usually several thoughts ahead of his time, believed that such a canal could not be realistically considered for at least a century. And yet the Erie Canal was built, just as its planners dreamed it would be; and it worked, just as its inexperienced builders believed it would.

For the first time in the history of the United States a cheap and fast route ran through the Appalachians, the mountain chain that had so effectively divided the West from the East of early America. With this breach, the fertile interior became accessible: the great inland lakes of America were linked to all the seas of the world.

Even now, long after railroads and turnpikes have generally replaced canals—including many the Erie inspired—and the old Erie itself has been superseded, the narrow waterway is still remembered. Stories and songs from the days when it was so heavily traveled, and paintings that capture the leisurely delights of a barge ride from Albany to Buffalo, have allowed the Erie to live on long after the closing of its last lock.

—The Editors

Two lamplighted canalboats glide along under the moon in this scene of nighttime traffic on the Erie in the 1830's.

COVER: *This 1884 scene of the Erie Canal shows a packet being towed around a bend, past a house clinging to a rocky slope near Little Falls.*

NEW-YORK HISTORICAL SOCIETY

ENDSHEETS: *The Erie Canal flows through sparsely settled country in the Mohawk Valley, closely following the course of the Mohawk River.*

CANAJOHARIE ART GALLERY

TITLE PAGE: *Sturdy tow horses pull a packet on a section of the Erie Canal near Little Falls, which appears in the background of this watercolor.*

This painted china plate, which was made about 1825, shows the Erie Canal joining the Hudson River near Albany.

CONTENTS

ILLUSTRATED WITH PAINTINGS, PRINTS, PHOTO-
GRAPHS, DRAWINGS, AND MAPS OF THE PERIOD

1 A NEW WAY WEST

During the summer of 1777 the American revolutionary army was retreating down the Hudson River before General Burgoyne's British redcoats and hired Hessians. Fort Ticonderoga had been outflanked and abandoned without a shot being fired; and the chances that the new American nation would last much longer looked very gloomy.

It hardly seemed a time to be talking about great plans for the future, especially something so vast as a canal to span the wilderness of upper New York. But that was exactly what Gouverneur Morris, a member of the First Continental Congress, chose to discuss one night during the retreat. Morris had come up to Fort Edward, north of Troy, to see how things were going with the ragged army. And one evening as mist settled over the northern forest and the air grew chill, he sat in a warm farmhouse kitchen with a group of officers and spoke of the future of the country.

Down the river below the retreating army, Morris told them, the Mohawk River joins the Hudson from the west. He painted a word-picture of a peaceful waterway which would extend from the Hudson, through the valley

Before the Erie Canal was opened, the journey west was long and arduous. Taking little but its livestock with them, this frontier family pauses briefly at a creek before pushing into the wilderness.

*This 1815 map shows that there were three tolerable routes across the moun-
tains for east–west travel. From north to south they were: The Great Genesee Road's Mohawk Turnpike, the National Road, and the Wilderness Road.*

of the Mohawk, all the way to Lake Erie. He spoke, according to one listener, of the day "when the waters of the great western inland seas would, by the aid of man, break through their barriers and mingle with those of the Hudson." These waters, Morris said, would carry an endless procession of boats bearing passengers and goods to and from the western territories of the new country by way of the Great Lakes.

Later, Morris wrote an exuberantly prophetic letter about such a waterway in which he said, "As yet, we only crawl along the outer shell of our country. The interior excels the part we inhabit in soil, in climate, in everything. The proudest empire in Europe is but a bubble compared to what America *will* be, *must* be, in the course of two centuries, perhaps of one." To Gouverneur Morris then, goes the honor of being one of the first men to consider seriously the tremendous potential of an inland waterway cutting across New York state. By connecting the Hudson River with Lake Erie, this waterway would breach at last the extensive mountain barrier that had divided the country. It would also effectively open up trade between the East and the West.

Four years after that visit the war for independence was won. People began heading for the western territories to find a piece of land of their own. And the stories they sent back East started the tide of emigration flowing. They told of land that raised

Gouverneur Morris was one of the first leading Americans to champion a waterway from the Hudson to Lake Erie to open the West.

a hundred bushels of corn to an acre; of hogs that grew wonderfully fat just rooting on acorns and beechnuts the forests provided at no cost to the settler; of the poorest families who "here adorn their tables three times a day like a wedding feast."

Men weary of fighting the rocks on thin-soiled hill farms in New England heard the call and headed west. So did men in the crowded cities who were tired to the bone of working for other men's pay with few prospects of getting ahead. But one saw no lines of covered wagons along this westward route, for most of the mountain crossing were trails just wide enough for a traveler on horseback, followed by a pack horse and perhaps two or three cattle.

The way west was difficult. The

OVERLEAF: *This is a view of the Mohawk Valley in 1866. The turbulent river's many rapids and falls made it nearly unnavigable.*

long chain of the Appalachian Mountains extending from Canada into Alabama formed a wall dividing the country in half. Eastern manufacturers had no way of shipping their goods to people living across the mountains except at tremendous cost. And faced with the same difficulties of transportation, the western farmers had no incentive to grow crops for the big eastern cities.

The great need was for a new and easy road through the mountains. But in all the hundreds of miles of mountain country between the gap cut by the St. Lawrence River, and Alabama, where the mountains dwindle away, there is only one real break—the valley where the Mohawk and the Hudson rivers meet.

The Hudson River part of the route was all a traveler could ask for; nature had made it deep and wide and calm, with little current. The Mohawk was another kettle of fish. It was dangerous in high water and impassable in low. Even when a boatman caught it right there were parts of the river a boat could never get through: there were swirling rapids, foaming waterfalls, and passages choked with rocks. This prevented the traveler who took a Hudson River boat to the juncture of the two rivers from changing to another boat to continue up the Mohawk. He had to load his family and possessions aboard a wagon at Albany, and then rattle for seventeen miles over the rough trail to Schenectady where the Mohawk became a

little tamer. There he hired a square-ended, flat-bottomed bateau and boatmen to pole them up the river.

At Little Falls everyone got out while the bateau was hauled around the waterfalls—people of the village earned a good part of their living performing that service for boatmen—then the backbreaking work of poling against the current began again. When the river became too small for the boat another wagon was hired, and the westbound family rattled overland to Lake Ontario. There they took another lake boat as far as the Niagara River, where there was more land travel to get around the falls and rapids. Then at Buffalo everybody piled aboard a Lake Erie boat and crossed into the west.

Yet, even with these tremendous difficulties, this was one of the favored ways to go west, and the number of people moving along it steadily increased. In 1792 the Western Inland Lock Navigation Company was formed to provide a way by water from the Hudson to Lake Ontario. At first, the company dug and blasted with a great deal of enthusiasm, but soon both money and enthusiasm were gone and the rough and rocky Mohawk River was not much changed. But the company managed to construct small locks around Little Falls, and to dig a narrow canal. This considerably eased the passage, for a boat could now pass from the Mohawk, through the chain of lakes in central and western New York, to within a

The road along the Mohawk River (above) was the best route through the northern Appalachians. Emigrants trying other routes had to cross the mountains on trails suitable only for stout mules and pack horses (below).

De Witt Clinton staked his career on the Erie. At first he favored it for political reasons, but it soon became his personal mission.

few miles of the Pennsylvania line.

The work was crude and only partly finished, but it gave a hint of what a real waterway along this route would mean. Before that time, bateaux with the capacity of one and one-half tons were the largest craft used on the Mohawk, simply because heavier boats could not be dragged around Little Falls. But with the locks, big ten-ton flatboats, called Durham boats, could easily be floated past the waterfalls. A bateau could carry only one emigrant family and their possessions, but several families along with their wagons, plows, kettles, and Bibles could ride on a Durham boat. As a result, boatmen were able to lower their fares. This further increased westward travel through the Mohawk Valley, and sparked interest in an even cheaper and easier route inland.

The Western Inland Lock Navigation Company, however, was not going to be the one to build that better way. The company had used every cent it had collected in tolls just to keep its shaky locks and channels in working condition. In eighteen years it had not been able to return a single penny to investors who had put their money into it expecting a good profit. Finally, in 1810, the company went to the state of New York for help, but was refused. A prominent politician named Jonas Platt had decided that it was time the state itself got things moving. He was hoping, as was Gouveneur Morris, to build a canal right across the state. The route to Lake Erie was longer, but it bypassed the Niagara barrier, and led directly into the West. To avoid the natural hazards of streams and rivers, he planned to build a totally artificial waterway.

The previous year, New York had sent two legislators to Washington to talk with President Jefferson about financial help from the federal government for the canal. They knew that Jefferson had proposed spending federal funds on building roads and canals, and they hoped to convince him of the importance of the Erie project. But Jefferson had a pet canal project of his own. He was thinking of the Potomac Company which had been formed in 1785 with George Washington as its president. They had planned to build a canal from Washington across the Appalachians to the Ohio River. But the company had run out of money after it had done no more than build a canal to bypass the worst of the Potomac rapids which foamed over rock ledges near Washington. Jefferson still cherished the hope that the early canal project might be finished. On the other hand, he felt that the proposed New York canal was too long and far too difficult to construct to be a practical idea in 1809. "It is a splendid project and may be executed a century hence," the President remarked to the two New Yorkers, ". . . but it is little short of madness to think of it at this day!"

Badly as the canal wanted federal funds, it needed a local champion

even more. The men who needed political support to get action on the
canal turned finally to a man named
De Witt Clinton. At that time, Clinton
was forty-three years old, mayor of
New York City, and the Democratic
leader of the state. He had served in
the state legislature and then in the
United States Senate before becoming
one of the most active mayors New
York City would ever have. When
there was a fire he arrived at the scene
behind his own galloping team almost
as soon as the first fire wagon, and he
showed up to help the police when
there was any disturbance. He was also
a member of many philosophical organizations, and an ardent naturalist.

The only trouble was that De Witt
Clinton had never been much inter-
ested in the canal, nor had he really
given much thought to it. But his chief
political opponent, Jonas Platt, who
had been lobbying for the canal, knew
that the project had little chance without Clinton's support. Fortunately,
Platt realized that the waterway was
more important than political maneu-
vering, and he suggested that Clinton
take the lead in backing it. Clinton
saw that such a move might be polit-
ically advantageous, and threw his
support behind the project. From that
time until his death, no one worked
harder for the canal than he did. In
fact, the Erie might never have been
dug if it had not been for the cease-
less efforts of De Witt Clinton.

A committee was appointed to
study the problems of digging the

canal. Clinton, of course, was made
one of the seven commissioners. And
so was Gouverneur Morris—getting a
little grey by now, but still vigorous
and full of ideas. The commissioners
traveled into the wilds of western New
York to look over the path of the
proposed canal. After this survey
they recommended that the waterway
run beside the Mohawk River only
as far as Utica and from there con-

tinue on to Lake Erie in its own path. The committee first suggested an inclined plane—a canal without locks which would slope gently downhill all the way from Lake Erie to Utica. This slope, they thought, would provide just enough slant to keep the water running and the channel full, but not enough to make it difficult to tow a boat against the current.

The inclined plane was Gouver-

Robert Fulton's steamboat the Paragon *(above), first began to ferry passengers up and down the Hudson as debate on an Erie canal came to a boil. Steam power was not used on canalboats, for the churning paddle wheels and powerful wakes would have wrecked the canal's earthen walls. But steam did speed up the trip from New York to Albany, where the canal would begin—if it were to exist at all. This painting of the* Paragon *was done about 1811, by a Russian artist who was as impressed with the variety of passengers as with the boat.*

Before the Erie, the longest canal in America was the Middlesex in Massachusetts (above), a technical success but a financial failure.

neur Morris's idea, but simple as it appeared, the plan proved too impractical to build. It would have required great embankments to carry it over the low places; and at one spot it would have needed a tremendous aqueduct 150 feet high to carry the waterway across a particularly low area.

Early in 1812 it was estimated that the construction of an inclined plane would cost between five and six million dollars—an exceptional sum in those days. Hopeful attempts to obtain loans in England and France were made, but they failed, and Morris's scheme was dropped. Then Clinton and the other commissioners sat down and started to work on plans for a canal with locks: this would be considerably cheaper to build than an inclined plane.

But the canal troubles of 1812 were not over yet, for the war with Great Britain broke out. This dimmed hopes for pushing the immediate construction of the canal. The war, however, did emphasize the need for a good waterway; the rotting old locks built by the Western Inland Lock Navigation Company could barely take care of the heavy war traffic.

Unfortunately, the war also gave the opposition time to gather its forces. New York City politicians stubbornly and stupidly opposed the upstate project although common sense should have told them that the commerce brought by the canal could only increase the greatness of their city. Then there were people in the Lake Ontario counties who wanted the canal to end at Oswego on Lake Ontario, instead of going on to Lake Erie and opening east–west traffic. And there were the farmers near the

One of the twenty locks on the Middlesex is shown being opened here. The canal also had seven aqueducts and was crossed by fifty bridges.

Pennsylvania border who saw no reason to pay taxes to help build a waterway so far away from them. But Clinton, always the master politician, promised to run branch canals into other parts of the state and soon had most of the farmers on his side.

People complained that there was not a chance in the world that a canal 363 miles long could be dug successfully through all that wilderness. Look, they said, at the Western Inland Lock Navigation Company which had tried to carry out a much less ambitious program, but had been able to complete only a small part of it before it went broke. Another sad example was the Middlesex Canal which ran twenty-seven miles from Boston to the Merrimack River; the longest canal in the country at that time. The Middlesex Canal was a marvel and a joy to shippers bring-

ing New Hampshire granite and lumber to Boston markets, but it was a nightmare to its owners who had to dig into their pockets again and again to pay off its debts. If a twenty-seven-mile canal near busy Boston went broke, asked the critics of the Erie, what chance had a ditch that would run hundreds of miles through the wilds of upper New York state?

But in spite of all the opposition, the pressure for the canal was becoming stronger all the time. New England farmers, thinking about taking up a piece of easily plowed land out in the Indiana or Illinois territories, were fascinated by the prospect of gliding along a smooth waterway rather than facing the difficulties of wearing out horses and axles on a miserable, potholed road over the mountains. Eastern merchants were ready to sell axes, buttons, plowpoints, cloth, fox traps,

OVERLEAF: *Much of New York state's political bickering about the canal occurred in the senate chamber, here comically viewed in 1850.*

and a thousand other things to western settlers as soon as economical transportation was available.

More vocal were the people in almost every town and village along the route of the proposed canal who, throughout 1816, were holding mass meetings to demand that the lawmakers in Albany get busy and do something. Many of the responsible citizens of New York City signed a petition asking for the same canal their own representatives were opposing. Thousands of people in other parts of the state also signed petitions for the canal. "Our tables have groaned with the petitions of these people," said a state senator, who originally opposed the canal. Then, in the spring of 1817, the people elected De Witt Clinton governor of New York by a vote of 43,310 to 1,479. It was the most lopsided vote the state had ever seen. And in voting for Clinton and his political allies, who had made the canal a major issue in their campaign, the people were really voting for the canal itself.

Later that year, when the all-important bill for funds to build the canal came up in the state legislature, its enemies still fought hard. Not until the final hour of the session did the bill come to a vote and pass.

But even then, the battle was not quite over. Under the rules of the New York Legislature, the bill had to be approved by a special group called the Council of Revision. Two of the five members were completely opposed to the idea of a canal; a third, James Kent, chief justice of the New York supreme court, thought the canal might be a fine thing some day—but not for a good many years in the future. The great waterway seemed doomed when Daniel Tompkins, the Vice President of the United States, walked into the meeting room of the divided council.

Tompkins was a former governor of New York and very much against the canal, which he considered a waste of money. Just to make sure the council would vote against the canal bill, he warned its members that there would be another war with England within two years, and that the state ought to be spending its money on weapons and fortifications, rather than for anything so foolish as the canal.

This was the worst thing he could have said. Judge Kent, who was going to vote against the canal bill, resented Tompkins's attempts to frighten the committee with talk of war. Rising from his seat, he announced, "If we must have war, or have a canal, I am in favor of the canal."

And so, by the margin of one vote, the Erie Canal was approved. It was one of the most important votes in American history. The crowd of people waiting outside in a hard April rain to hear the decision knew how important it was and cheered again and again when they received word of the final vote.

Now the job was up to the men with axes and picks and shovels.

The Erie Canal would undoubtedly benefit New York City. The view above shows Manhattan, the Hudson, and the busy East River in 1837.

OVERLEAF: *Having crossed the Appalachians, these emigrants glide down the Ohio on a barge steered by two men on an outboard rudder.*

2 DIGGING THE DITCH

In the wilderness village of Rome, on July 4, 1817, the great western canal at last got under way with a ceremony to mark the turning of the first shovelfuls of earth.

Dignitaries made speeches there that day, after which they walked over to the stakes marking the line of the canal, and each in turn took a bright new spade and turned over a bit of earth. The crowd of onlookers cheered, cannons boomed, the crowd cheered again, and construction on the great canal was at last officially begun. Now the real work could start.

Rome, at first glance, might seem an odd place to start digging a canal. It was out on the edge of nowhere, with only three or four tiny settlements and a tremendous amount of wilderness between it and Lake Erie to the west. And there was a considerable amount of wilderness to the east as well. Materials and tools would have to be hauled into Rome over difficult trails and waterways, or fashioned on the spot. But it was the town nearest the upper limit of navigation on the Mohawk River. It was also right at the middle section of the canal where the digging would be the easiest. There was little rock to

Clearing frontier farmland was rugged, backbreaking work, as this 1825 landscape suggests. It took daring, vision, and dogged perseverance to clear hundreds of miles of wilderness for a waterway.

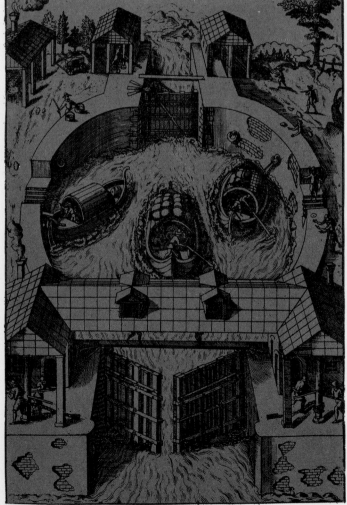

To overcome natural obstacles in the path of a canal, Europeans gradually developed two indispensable devices—the lock and the aqueduct. Below left is a drawing of an early lock in Italy where the technique of controlling the water level to raise or lower boats was first used. A seventeenth-century sketch shows water rushing out of an oval basin where three boats are being lowered to a new level. Above is an English aqueduct, or water-carrying bridge, for the eighteenth-century Bridgewater Canal. A full-rigged boat, pulled by two horses, glides along, high above the river that the aqueduct had been built to span.

The cross section (right) of a riverside portion of the Erie Canal shows its dimensions, and the location of the towpath and berm—the bank across from the towpath.

cut through at Rome, and it was level country where no locks would be needed. Clinton and the other canal commissioners felt it was important to make good progress at the beginning, to have something to show the people as soon as possible. If they had begun work from the Hudson River end, they would have had to blast through rocks and build locks from the start. In spite of all the blueprints and brave talk, no one knew enough about canal building yet to begin on such a difficult part.

From end to end, Hudson River to Lake Erie, the canal would be 363 miles long. The channel was to be forty feet wide at the surface, and would slope inward to twenty-eight feet at the bottom; the water in the channel would be four feet deep. Besides these basic requirements, the engineers would have to consider that Lake Erie is 568 feet higher than the Hudson River. There were also places where the canal would step down to cross a broad valley and then rise up again on the other side. So, counting steps up and down, the total vertical distance a boat would travel on the canal would be 688 feet. Eighty-three locks would have to be built to overcome these differences in height (see chart, page 36).

There were other problems: American canalboats had neither sails nor oars and needed to be towed. So, along the length of the canal there would be a towpath ten feet wide for the horses and mules which were needed to draw the canalboats. Few sections of the Erie Canal could run through any existing stream, and uncontrollable natural waterways had to be avoided completely. Where the channel ran next to the Mohawk River, it would be carefully protected from it by walls and dikes. These and a thousand other things had to be planned carefully before the first shovelful of earth could be turned.

As though these engineering feats

DRAWING BY CAL SACKS

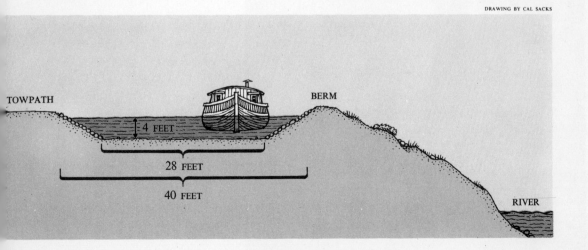

TOWPATH   BERM   RIVER

4 FEET

28 FEET

40 FEET

were not enough, the legislature of New York also approved the digging of a canal from Lake Champlain to the Hudson River. It would join the Erie Canal near the Hudson end of their courses where the combined traffic would move down to Albany and on to the Hudson River. Cautious men shook their heads at the mounting costs, while Clinton's political enemies grinned slyly and then sat back to wait for the whole mad canal scheme to collapse and bury Clinton's political hopes once and for all.

But up around Rome, activity on the Erie Canal was well under way. First the surveyors had staked out a sixty-foot-wide path to be cleared of trees. Within this they set two rows of stakes forty feet apart to mark the actual channel. Next came the axemen to clear the sixty-foot swath. This was truly a job for the legendary woodsman, Paul Bunyan. The men had to clear mile after mile of woods, and fell trees, many of which were seven or eight feet in diameter.

Once the trees and brush were down and burned, the crews with shovels had their turn. These men had to dig through a tangled mass of roots which nature had been weaving into a nearly impregnable barrier for centuries. It not only took

Where the path of the canal ran through heavily wooded areas, countless trees had to be cut down. This scene shows two men clearing the wilderness in the time-honored manner—with strong arms and ringing axes.

34

courage to face such difficulties, but a touch of madness as well, for no one then had had any real experience in building such a canal.

Not just experience was lacking; there was no precedent in all history for a canal of the Erie's length. Canal building was a young and undeveloped art. True, it had been practiced by the Egyptians. They had constructed canals of up to 125 miles in length before the birth of Christ; but these generally ran over level terrain, involved a ruthless expenditure of human life, and were often little more than impermanent ditches. What knowledge the Egyptians, and later the Romans, acquired in the building of canals was buried, as were most of the canals themselves, in the Middle Ages. Only in the seventeenth century, with the development of the locks in Italy, was the art revived, and then the first true ancestors of the Erie Canal were born.

The largest European canal to grow out of the revival was the Languedoc Canal that cut across southern France, connecting the Atlantic with the Mediterranean. Its 144 miles, still in operation, have 119 locks, and are a complex of aqueducts and tunnels as well as channels. Opened in 1681, the French canal was still considered a marvel of modern engineering when the Erie's planners were brashly contemplating a canal two and a half times as long!

The rash of canals built in England in the second half of the eighteenth century inspired the planners as much as the Languedoc. An English engineer, who had gained his experience in this building spree, had been hired by the Western Lock Navigation Company to aid their abortive efforts to build a canal linking the Hudson and Lake Ontario. The Erie commissioners tried to get the same engineer for their ambitious undertaking, but he turned down their job offer. So the commissioners selected as chief engineers two New York lawyers, Benjamin Wright and James Geddes, whose only previous experience had been a little bit of surveying work they had done in connection with legal work involving property boundaries. Though Wright and Geddes were not engineers by profession, the commissioners felt that the two men were competent and intelligent enough to solve the problems of canal construction on the job. In the end, the commissioners turned out to be right.

Finding workers for the canal was no problem. Men came from miles around, eager to make some of the big money being paid for diggers on the Big Ditch. The actual hiring was done by small contractors who agreed to dig a certain length of channel for a certain price. Then it was up to the contractor to hire the men to do the work. He was also expected to put up a shack big enough to sleep twenty-four to forty men; to supply them with horses, scrapers, shovels, and other equipment; to feed them and give them their daily ration of

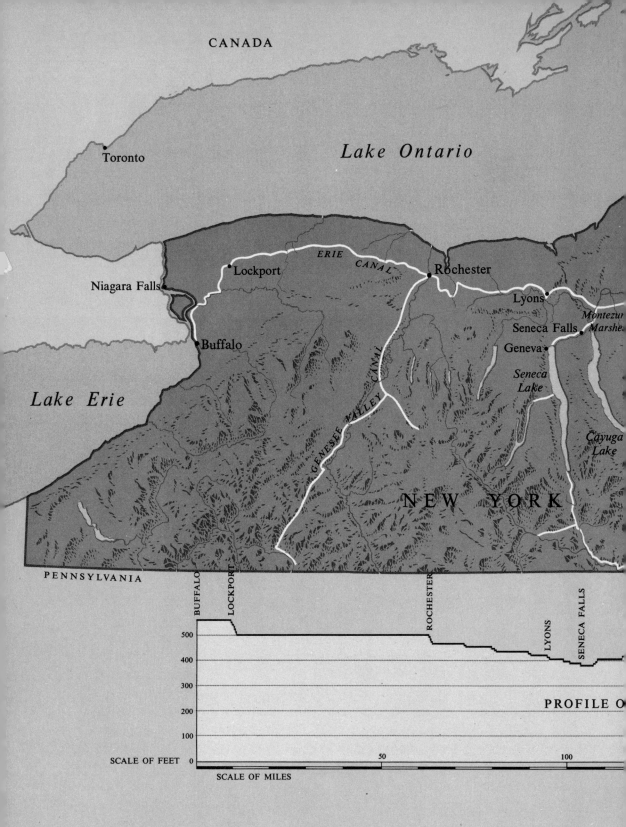

CANADA

Toronto

Lake Ontario

ERIE   CANAL

Lockport   Rochester

Niagara Falls   Lyons

Seneca Falls   *Montezur*
                                                        Marshe
Buffalo   Geneva

Lake Erie   *Seneca*
                                                    Lake

GENESEE VALLEY   CANAL

Cayuga
Lake

NEW   YORK

PENNSYLVANIA

BUFFALO LOCKPORT   ROCHESTER   LYONS SENECA FALLS

500

400

300   PROFILE O

200

100

SCALE OF FEET 0   50   100

SCALE OF MILES

ROUTE OF THE ERIE CANAL

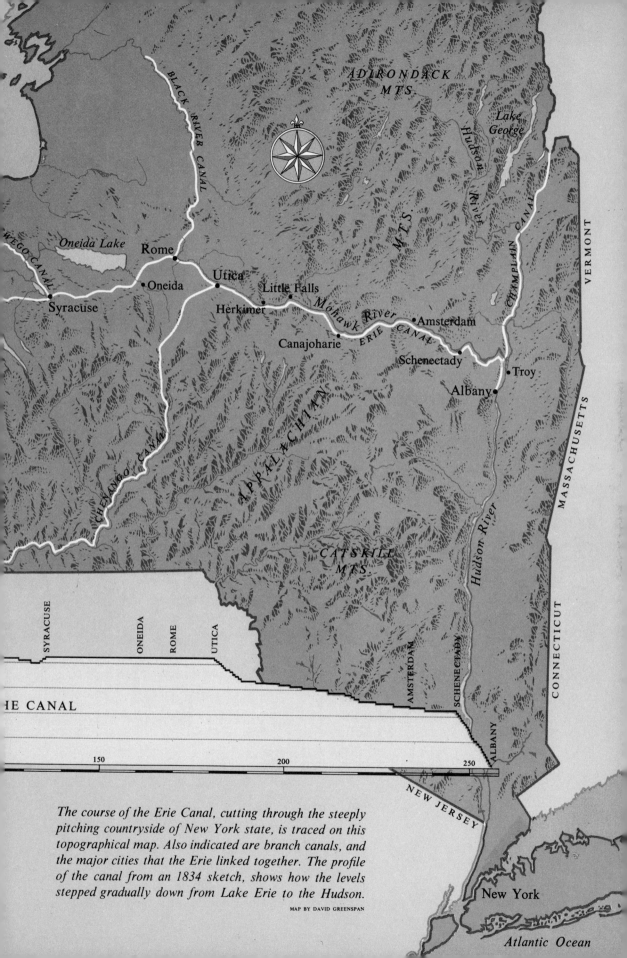

ADIRONDACK
MTS.

Lake
George

BLACK RIVER CANAL

HUDSON RIVER

MTS.

CHAMPLAIN CANAL

VERMONT

Oneida Lake

OSWEGO CANAL

Rome

Oneida

Syracuse

Utica

Herkimer

Little Falls

Canajoharie

Mohawk River

ERIE CANAL

Amsterdam

Schenectady

Troy

Albany

CHENANGO CANAL

APPALACHIANS

CATSKILL
MTS.

Hudson River

MASSACHUSETTS

CONNECTICUT

SYRACUSE

ONEIDA

ROME

UTICA

AMSTERDAM

SCHENECTADY

ALBANY

THE CANAL

150

200

250

NEW JERSEY

*The course of the Erie Canal, cutting through the steeply
pitching countryside of New York state, is traced on this
topographical map. Also indicated are branch canals, and
the major cities that the Erie linked together. The profile
of the canal from an 1834 sketch, shows how the levels
stepped gradually down from Lake Erie to the Hudson.*

MAP BY DAVID GREENSPAN

New York

Atlantic Ocean

Among the builders of the Erie were two lawyers who served as the chief engineers —Benjamin Wright (far left), and James Geddes (left)—and some three thousand Irishmen. One of these sturdy laborers is seen at right, making a final check on a sailing notice. He is about to go from Dublin to New York and, he hopes, from rags to riches.

whiskey; and to pay them. Wages were as high as eighty cents a day.

But with everyone shouting for more speed, the supply of native American workers was not enough. Recruiters were sent down to New York City, to meet the immigrant boats arriving from Ireland. "Would they care for a fine job upstate?" the recruiters asked the husky young Irishmen. "We're digging a canal up there," they explained. "Working conditions are very good, with roast beef guaranteed twice a day, regular whiskey rations, and wages eighty cents." This was nearly twice as much as most unskilled laborers were earning in America at that time, and three times as much as unskilled immigrant laborers could have earned in Europe. By 1825, wages rose to a dollar a day. The Irish were ready to take almost any work, but they wanted to make sure they had heard right. Those wages, they asked, they would be eighty cents a week, of course. When the men found it was eighty cents a day, it would have been impossible

to keep them away from the Erie with clubs. The first of the Irish laborers arrived in 1818, and during the digging of the canal they made up about a quarter of the work force. The remainder of the laborers hired were other European immigrants and native-born Americans.

Everyone worked long, hard hours around the construction sites. In the Erie work camps, the wake-up horn was blown by the cook's helper half an hour before sunrise; he followed the blast with the call, "All out! Mush in the kettle!" There was more than mush though because breakfast offered most of these items: fried eggs, steak, sausage or pork chops, ham, potatoes, corn bread, rolls, batter cakes with molasses, buckwheat cakes with syrup, fried mush or mush-and-milk, and tea, coffee, or buttermilk. It took a lot of fuel to stoke up a man for canal digging. He put it away in a hurry and was at work by sunup.

The kitchen crew packed hearty lunches that the men carried along, and they ate at noon during a half-hour

38

These pencil sketches by the frontier artist
Joshua Shaw show (above) the three-wheeled,
horse-drawn wheelbarrow used for hauling
heavy material when the canal was built, and
(below) woodsmen at work with their axes.

break. At night they came in a little before sundown ready for a big supper. Game of every kind, from venison and bear to squirrel and partridge, was plentiful along the canal route, but the workers quickly tired of this woodland fare and demanded beef, pork, and mutton. Most contractors had to promise the men they hired that game would never be served to them more than a certain number of days in the week.

During the long days of summer a work day might last as long as fourteen hours; after that even a hard, board bunk probably felt good although the sleeping shacks provided scant comfort. There was no glass or screening on the windows and every mosquito within miles could come and fill up on a canal-digger's blood. The two-tiered bunks had no mattresses and if a worker wanted bedding he brought his own. The men had a saying: "Hickory lasts longer, but pine sleeps softer."

As the newness of the life wore off and the men got into the rhythm of their work, they sang a song of their own about the canal they were digging:

We are cutting a Ditch through the
    gravel,
Through the gravel across the state,
    by heck!
We are cutting the Ditch through the
    gravel,
So the people and the freight can
    travel,
Can travel across the state, by heck!

And as they sang, the work began to go faster and more smoothly than it had at the beginning. Engineers and men alike had learned about canal building from scratch, but they learned fast. Yankee ingenuity quickly showed them how to lick problems that at first had made them shudder. Their only sources of power were the muscles of men, horses, and oxen, so they devised ways to increase their efficiency without adding to their work load. Those giant trees for instance— it was not very long before they had one man pulling them over. Someone had devised a technique whereby a chain was tied high in a tree with the other end leading to a wheel worked by an endless-screw gear. As a man wound the gear with a crank, the tree was very slowly pulled over with irresistible force. This not only pulled down the tree, but yanked out the roots as well.

Stumps still in the earth from previously cleared land remained a problem until some unsung genius came up with a stump-pulling device that was as effective as it was simple. It had two tremendous wheels, sixteen feet in diameter, on the ends of a very sturdy axle thirty feet long. Fixed at the center of the axle was a slightly smaller wheel, fourteen feet in diameter, with a broad rim which held a coiled rope. This strange-looking machine was hauled into place so it straddled the stump, and the big outer wheels were tied down to hold it steady. A chain wound around the

axle was tied to the stump. A team of horses was hitched to the end of a rope wound around the rim of the middle wheel. Then as the animals strained, the rope grew taut, and made the center wheel rotate. This moved the axle which, in turn, wound up the chain which was fastened to the stump. The difference in size of wheel and axle multiplied the force tremendously, and the stump came out of the ground with a snapping and popping of roots as neatly as could be. Seven men and two horses could pull thirty to forty stumps in one day with this rig.

In such ingenious ways, the problems of making a canal were met and conquered—and the rate of progress improved steadily. Frequently on hand to see that things kept moving was De Witt Clinton. He tried to get away from his duties as governor as often as possible, to travel up to the canal to see how the work was coming. Clinton claimed that his promise to have the Big Ditch finished in 1823 still held; but his enemies guffawed, and even his friends urged him not to make such rash statements.

At one point it looked as though the canal was going to be stopped dead long before 1823. At first the middle section had been selected largely because it seemed to be the easiest digging, but one part of it turned out to be a nightmare. Near the section's west end, at the outlet of Cayuga Lake, was a low, marshy area across which the line of the canal

These cartoons from an old map of the Erie lampoon types of people seen around the canal: the dandified surveyors (above); the prosperous Dutch farmer and his disgruntled hired hand (below); and the "greenhorn," the bumpkin Irish laborer (right).

was to run for four and half miles. The Montezuma Marshes, named after a small village on their edge, were a dismal spot with impenetrable thickets of rushes taller than a man, and oozy black muck underfoot.

The first day in the marshes, the men joked about the easy digging. But the next morning their jokes had turned sour because the soft mud they had shoveled out had settled and flowed back into the ditch. There was little sign of the channel dug the day before. So, to keep the sides of the canal firm, they constructed retaining walls of planks held in place by long stakes driven down through the soft mud and into the firm layer of clay beneath. That worked pretty well, except that occasionally a man would pound a stake through the mire into the clay only to watch it sink into bottomless quicksand.

Even the Irishmen, who had shown a knack for working in swampy places, did not like this spot. Their legs swelled from standing in the water for hours, and leeches fastened onto them. But their sense of humor stayed with them and they gave such names to the worst places as "Bottomless Pit," "Digger's Misery," "Backbreak Bog," and "Mudturtles' Delight." They also added to their song:

We are digging the Ditch through the
     mire;
Through the mud and the slime and
     the mire, by heck!
And the mud is our principal hire;

DRAWING BY ANTHONY RAVIELLI

The giant device above was designed to remove stubborn tree stumps. The team of horses hauls a rope coiled on the central wheel; this turns the axle, tightens the chain, and uproots the stump. At left, men are seen years later working on the Erie's stumpless banks.

In our pants, up our sleeves, down
     our neck, by heck!
The mud is our principal hire.

But the worst did not come until early summer brought the mosquito season. The insects, enormous clouds of them, fell on the men in such savage numbers that hands swelled and eyes were puffed almost shut. Little smudge pots were obtained for the men which contained a small glowing fire covered with green leaves to create dense smoke. They were worn around the neck, and the men were soon calling them "Montezuma necklaces."

One of the pests that was making life so miserable was the anopheles mosquito, the carrier of malaria—although no one yet connected the insect with the disease. By early August, workers by the hundreds were coming down with chills and fevers. Almost every man able to walk left the job and got away because it was believed that bad air caused the sickness. A traveler passing through found a doctor working himself hollow-eyed caring for his hundreds of patients night and day. His first treatments had done little for the men, as they included bleeding, and the administration of feverwort, snakeroot, green pigweed, and Seneca Oil (known as petroleum in later years). He also tried a new drug from Peru called "Jesuit's Bark" and found that it seemed to do some good. In fact, the bark contained quinine

45

which later was recognized as the best treatment for malaria.

Soon, work in the Montezuma Marshes stopped completely and there was dark talk about giving up the whole project. But when the autumn came, the sickness disappeared with the mosquitoes—and the work went ahead once again. One of the bridges across the marshes was a marvel of the Big Ditch. It was a wooden structure built on stone piles which spanned some 1,300 feet of marshy ground.

Work on one vital and extensive part of the canal went on almost unknown to most people because it was done miles from the Erie itself. It was for the vital feeder system which supplied the canal with water. The slightly downward slope of the canal, which dropped from Lake Erie to the Hudson River, created a very gentle eastward flow of its water. This flow, together with continual evaporation and leakage of the canal's water, meant it had to be replenished all along the way. And so, while the Big Ditch itself was being dug, there was construction on a complex system of feeder channels and dammed streams to utilize the resources of all the nearby rivers and creeks. This system would bring water to the Erie under the control of sluice gates and waste gates which regulated the flow into the canal. Some of the feeder channels had a double purpose; they were to carry boats, and in time formed a small system of branch canals which opened up trade with farms and settlements hundreds of miles away from the centers of commerce.

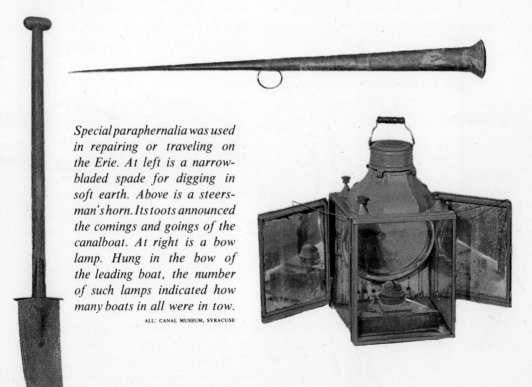

Special paraphernalia was used in repairing or traveling on the Erie. At left is a narrow-bladed spade for digging in soft earth. Above is a steersman's horn. Its toots announced the comings and goings of the canalboat. At right is a bow lamp. Hung in the bow of the leading boat, the number of such lamps indicated how many boats in all were in tow.
ALL: CANAL MUSEUM, SYRACUSE

In October of 1819, a little more than two years after the first ground-breaking ceremony at Rome, another crowd gathered there to celebrate the opening of the first stretch of canal. It was not much of a channel, extending only fifteen miles between Rome and Utica, but the commissioners had decided that something was needed to call attention to the progress that had been made. People wanted a canal, but when it was not dug overnight they became impatient. Clinton, who had been swept into the governor's office so overwhelmingly two years before, had become very unpopular by 1819. A piece of finished canal might convince the people that the Erie was coming right along, and that Clinton and the other commissioners had been on the job.

The sluice gates were opened and water rushed into the channel from the west. A spanking new boat, the *Chief Engineer of Rome*, became the first to float on Erie water. It was towed by a span of handsome horses from Rome to Utica in one day, and back the next. The event was celebrated with the usual speechmaking, firing of cannon, and hurrahing. Enemies of the governor and the canal sneered that at the rate of fifteen miles every two years, it would take forever to build the Erie. But considerably more than that had been done. Just about all the ninety-four miles of the middle section had been cleared, forty-eight of this had been dug, and another eight-mile length was ready for travel as soon as the inspectors checked it. Things were

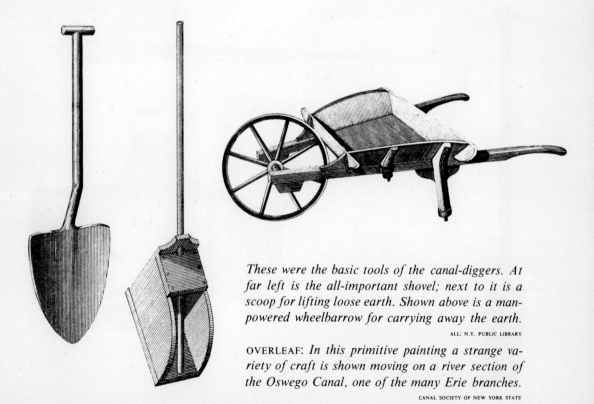

These were the basic tools of the canal-diggers. At far left is the all-important shovel; next to it is a scoop for lifting loose earth. Shown above is a man-powered wheelbarrow for carrying away the earth.

ALL: N.Y. PUBLIC LIBRARY

OVERLEAF: *In this primitive painting a strange variety of craft is shown moving on a river section of the Oswego Canal, one of the many Erie branches.*

CANAL SOCIETY OF NEW YORK STATE

progressing steadily on the Erie Canal.

That first fifteen-mile stretch immediately began to play an important part in the great westward migration; but for the people living beside it, it became a new and fascinating plaything. Almost every canalside dweller built himself a boat to float on the Erie. Most were jerry-built vessels, and many leaked badly. As often as not they finally settled to the bottom where the owner let them rest. Farmers found the channel very convenient for floating logs from one part of their farms to another, but they had the bad habit of leaving the logs in the channel for several days until they got around to hauling them out. The canal also developed into a fine place for fishing. The towpath was used for a road, and some of the more sporting-minded farmers even used it as a race track of an evening. At times the path was so cluttered with straying barnyard animals that a team towing a canalboat on honest business had a hard time getting through. Finally, a fence was built to keep the wandering animals off the towpath.

The canalboat captains complained bitterly about all this sort of activity. More than one of them had had his boat spring a leak after smashing against a sunken ark abandoned by some backwoods bumpkin who had grown tired of playing at being a canalman. The commissioners did set up a system of fines—five dollars for throwing rubbish into the channel,

ten dollars for leaving a sunken boat, etc.—but it was not strictly enforced. The commissioners did not want to make enemies of the countryfolk at a time when the canal needed every possible friend.

The same canalboat captains who demanded strict controls as far as the country people were concerned, sang another tune when tolls were put into effect. Some of them muffled

As a canalboat glides peacefully past some of upper New York state's rugged scenery, the cook hands the steersman his lunch. The top-hatted laborers in the foreground make necessary repairs to the Erie's towpath. Hundreds of workmen were kept busy repairing and enlarging the canal many years after it opened.

the feet of their horses by wrapping them in cloths and tried to sneak by the toll stations at night without paying. But the toll collector at Rome made a network of iron chains that he could lower into the water with a winch when night fell. After he caught a few boats trying to slip by his station, the practice of toll-dodging on the first small length of the Erie Canal came to an end.

51

Six years after the first stretch of Erie water was opened at Rome, Governor Clinton (standing proudly in the bow of the garlanded boat seen below) led a triumphal procession down the completed waterway.

DE WITT CLINTON HIGH SCHOOL; COURTESY OF MARGARET YARDLEY VOELKER

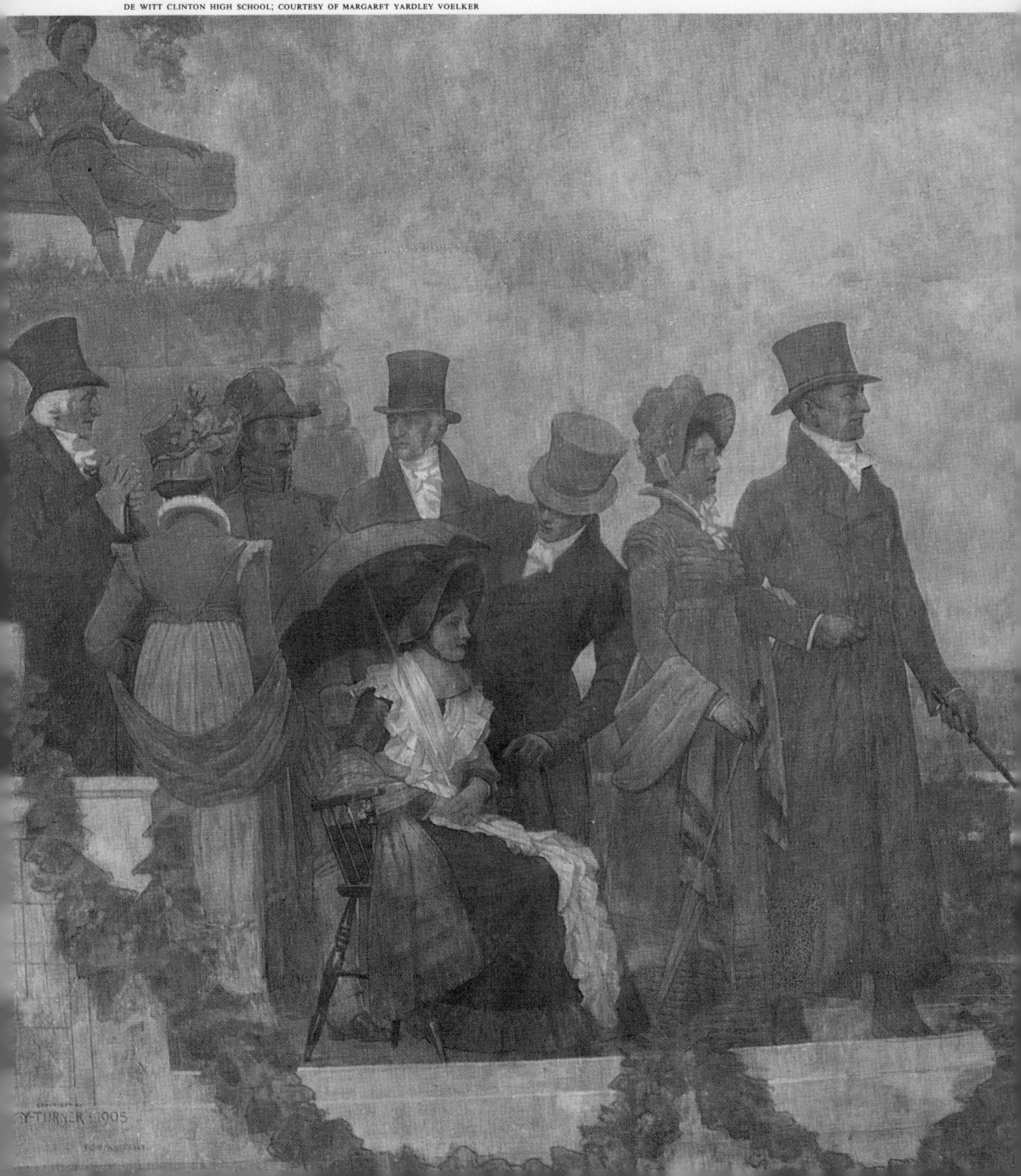

3 CLINTON'S TRIUMPH

Clinton's enemies scoffed when the first fifteen-mile stretch of canal was opened. Fifteen miles out of 363, now wasn't that something to boast about! Fifteen miles in two years! "Clinton's Ditch" was a mad project that would never be finished. It was sure to run the state far into debt if it was not stopped.

"Clinton's Ditch" became a nickname that would later be used with affection, but midway through the building of the canal it was a taunt. Troubles were piling up: towns which the canal bypassed were lobbying for a change of route; construction was moving much slower than most people had expected; and no revenues had come in yet from the opened stretches of canal. Nothing seemed to go smoothly for Clinton even though he soon gave the state plenty of canal.

The next year, 1820, water was admitted from the reserve basins into one part after another of the Erie. On the fourth of July, seventy-three fine new canalboats left Syracuse in a parade with speechmaking and fireworks to mark the completion of nearly all the middle section. The celebration had barely ended before the same boats were at work hauling produce, merchandise, and travelers along the newly opened canal route.

But even this progress did not bring back Clinton's fading popularity. The tide of public opinion was running too strongly against him. On election day in 1820 he barely retained his office, polling only 2,000 more votes than his opponent. Along with this setback, Clinton had to announce that he could not meet his campaign promise to have the canal finished by 1823. Difficulties had arisen, he said, and progress had been slower than expected. But he promised that it definitely would be ready for business by 1825. Once again there was an uproar from his enemies who said that the Ditch would not be finished in 1825 or any other year.

The criticism, however, did not stop the governor. He was much too busy pushing his crews even to consider failure. Except for the crossing of the Montezuma Marshes, the middle section had presented no other major engineering problems. But the builders found themselves facing one tough problem after another as they went to work on the eastern and western sections. Much of the land was rough and hilly, with deep valleys crossing the canal route. There was much rock to be blasted out. And almost all of the canal's eighty-three locks still had to be built to compensate for the long rise from the Hudson River to Lake Erie.

Where the route of a canal runs along level ground, construction can proceed smoothly. If a river crosses its course, the engineering need not be too difficult. In some cases a bridge for the towpath can easily be built, and the canalboats towed across the river. In other cases, particularly where a river's water is seasonally higher or lower than the canal, simple guard locks can be built to keep the river from flooding or clogging the canal. Hilly country, however, is consistently troublesome for canal builders.

And it was hilly country that Clinton's engineers began cutting through in 1820. Streams that lay in the way were usually in deep valleys much lower than the canal. The only way to get the waterway across was to put it on an aqueduct, as water-carrying bridges were called.

Many of the aqueducts were amazing works for their time. Most were of stone-arch construction, but others consisted of stone piers supporting trough-like wooden structures which carried the canal across the valley. The men who were surveying the lower Mohawk River for level terrain were forced to shift the route of the waterway back and forth across the river several times.

Two of the aqueducts that carried the Erie on these crossings were architectural marvels. The one below Schenectady was probably the most famous. Twenty-six stone piers carried it for 1,188 feet. Another, at Little Falls, was 744 feet long and

Bridges were constructed everywhere along the Erie. Great stone aqueducts, such as the one at Little Falls (above), carried the canal across valleys and over rivers. Hundreds of more humble, wooden spans (below) linked farms or roads which the Erie had cut.

spanned the river with three huge stone arches thirty feet high.

There were many more aqueducts along the Erie, and a number of them had their special claims to fame because of height or ingenuity of construction. The one at Rochester was the longest stone-arch bridge in the world when built: it was 802 feet long and had nine Roman arches which soared high above the turbulent Genesee River. But alas, this noble structure leaked badly, and had such a narrow channel that boats could not pass on it. Many legendary battles occurred here between crews of canalboats which had entered from opposite sides at about the same time, and claimed the right of way when they met in the middle. The bridge was replaced after ten years with a wider one that did not leak.

While the busy crews built world-famous aqueducts without benefit of power machinery, they also put up about 300 small bridges. A few were for country roads that the canal cut across, but most were for farmers whose lands had been split by the waterway. The state of New York had promised that it would build "occupation bridges" (so called because they allowed the owners to continue their occupation of farming) wherever their land was cut. To save money, the bridges were made low— only seven and a half feet above water.

The new tricks of aqueduct and bridge building that the crews and engineers had to learn were nothing to what faced them in the matter of building locks. Fifty-three locks had to be constructed in the hundred-mile stretch between Albany and Schenectady. Far to the west, the engineers were working at the biggest problem of all—how to get the canal up the steep rock face at Lockport.

And there was another grave problem in the east at Little Falls, where the old Western Inland Lock Navigation Company had once done so much for travel on the Mohawk River. The earlier builders had constructed locks to take the river traffic around the falls—and had spent several years doing it. The Erie Canal planners, however, brought their waterway up the opposite side of the river—ignoring the battered old locks and channel. They asked a consulting engineer for an opinion on how long it would take to hack a new channel through the solid rock and to build a set of locks. He looked over the situation, checked the plans, inspected the rock, and made a number of calculations. "Three years," he said. They thanked him, and paid his fee. Then they brought in their own crack crews and hired some hard-rock miners to teach them how to use explosives. In less than three months the channel was dug, although it took somewhat longer to finish the locks.

They were working in rock very often now, and the laborers had added still another verse to their song about building the Big Ditch:

COLDEN, *Memoir*, 1825

Waterfalls blocked the narrow Mohawk Valley at Little Falls, but the canal's builders overcame them with five locks and an aqueduct.

We are cutting the Ditch through the rocks,
Through the rocks across the state, by heck!
We are cutting the Ditch through the rocks,
And we'll finish her off with stone locks,
From the rocks across the state, by heck!
From the rocks across the state.

In the meantime, De Witt Clinton might have been getting things done on the construction of the canal, but he was still having his troubles elsewhere. In 1822 the anti-canal factions combined against him were so strong that he did not receive the nomination for governor. However, he was still a canal commissioner and continued to push the project that had become the one absorbing interest of his life.

At Buffalo, the Erie's western end, the canal ran beside the Niagara River until it emptied into Lake Erie as seen in this 1871 view.

But now opposition was coming not only from politicians and crackpots, but many of the taxpayers as well. The costs of the canal were mounting frighteningly. Several millions of dollars had been spent and some people were honestly convinced that when the canal was finished, it would never pay for itself. Surely it would be better to drop it now than to go on eternally paying its debts.

Clinton, knowing that time was growing short, worked feverishly. He urged his men on, settled problems, and saw that equipment and materials were on hand when and where they were needed. Regularly, from time to time, sluice gates leading from reservoirs and feeder channels were opened to let water into still another length of canal. By midsummer of 1822 the Erie was carrying water all along the 280 miles of its projected route. And just before the fall freeze-up put an end to work that year, boats were also operating between Little Falls and Schenectady. Clinton's Ditch had become the biggest ditch anyone had ever seen.

Then, in April of 1824, Clinton's political enemies felt that they were strong enough to move against the

The eastern end of the canal was at Albany whose Dutch origins are apparent in the steeply pitched roofs of the houses pictured above.

champion of the canal and the people. They stripped him of his one remaining office—the one that really counted. He was removed from his position as a canal commissioner, an office he had held since 1810.

There were hundreds of canal proposals before the state legislature: these suggested changing the course of the canal, or finishing only one section rather than all the waterway, or stopping funds for locks. For a frightening moment it looked as though the anti-canal forces might be able to stop work entirely on the Erie.

But Clinton's political enemies had gone too far. Financial reports on the toll collections coming in showed that travelers were eagerly using what there was of the Erie, even though they had to haul their goods by wagon around the unopened sections. Some 1,822 boats were operating on one stretch only forty-five miles long, out beyond the growing wilderness village of Rochester. On this section alone almost $21,000 in tolls had been collected in six months. By the end of the summer, the total collected by all operating sections of the canal was almost $300,000. Those who had opposed Clinton because they honestly

These photographs show the famous sets of locks for which Lockport was named. A boat is descending the left-hand, eastbound locks above; the right-hand set was for rising, westbound traffic. Below, some of the workers who tended the locks pose on the balance beams.

believed the canal would always be a money-loser began to feel that Clinton had been treated unjustly and threw their support behind him.

So once again De Witt Clinton was back in favor, and when the November elections came around he was nominated for the governorship and elected by a comfortable majority of 103,000 to 87,000. The new governor at once announced that, in spite of the time he had lost, the canal was still going to be ready by autumn of 1825 —less than a year away!

The remaining major projects were finished in good time. The twenty-seven locks in the rocky climb from Albany to Schenectady were completed, and at last it was possible to travel between the two cities by water. Far in the other direction, near the western end of the canal, crews worked frantically to finish up the great engineering work known as the Lockport Five.

At Lockport, north of Buffalo, there was a sharp change in the level of the rocky land which became almost a cliff. Nathan Roberts, another of the Erie's self-made engineers, had pondered long about how he was going to get the canal up that rock face. With no one to help him, and no guidance except a few books, he designed a double set of five locks—one set for eastbound and another for westbound travel. This was the only place on the Erie where there were two sets of locks. They were needed to avoid hopeless bottlenecks; other-

Nathan S. Roberts built the locks which brilliantly conquered Lockport's rock wall. He considered the acceptance of his design the most triumphant moment of his career.

wise, a boat going one way would have had to pass through all five locks before a boat coming the other way could start through. Each lock had a lift of twelve feet instead of the usual eight feet four inches, and were cut out of solid rock—even the towpath. At one point on their shelflike path, horses and driver were a dizzy sixty feet above the lock.

Lockport's amazing system of locks was completed in June of 1825; and a few months later, water was admitted to the westernmost 140 miles of the canal. This section of the Erie involved deep cutting, frequently through solid

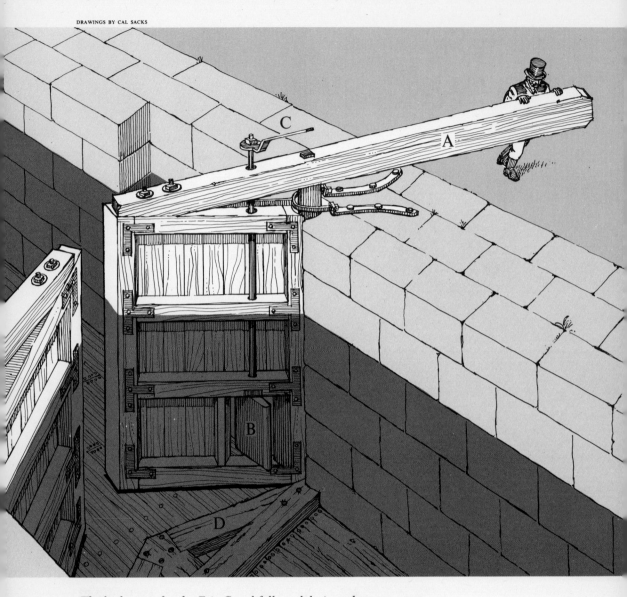

The lock gates for the Erie Canal followed designs that were centuries old in their basic engineering. Shown above is an Erie-type gate and its major components: the balance beam (A), which opened or closed the main gate; the sluice gate (B) and sluice gate control (C) which permitted water to flow slowly into or out of a lock so a boat could be raised or lowered to the level of the water outside the exit gate; and the mitre sill (D), against which the gate was locked and sealed. The drawings at right show a lock in action. A barge enters through the upstream gates which are then closed; the water flows out through a sluice in the downstream gates, lowering the boat to a new level; then it emerges into the channel.

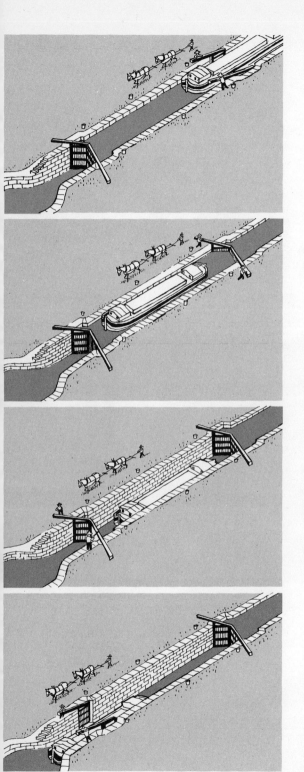

rock, between Buffalo and Lockport to keep the canal's level below that of Lake Erie. With such cutting, the lake became an inexhaustible water supply for the western end of the canal. A gentle flow of lake water moved continually from Buffalo to Lockport. In this section the Erie dropped approximately one inch for each of the twenty-five miles of waterway which ran from Buffalo to Lockport. This gradual incline, and the deep cuts as well, were objects of almost as much admiration by foreign engineers as the two sets of locks themselves.

The western end of the Erie Canal was the last section to be finished. With its completion, the entire canal was about ready to open. Still, as Clinton's promised deadline approached, a small number of unfinished details remained. The supervisors and crews hurried to take care of the most important ones. They built three weighlocks at Troy, Utica, and Syracuse in which boats would be weighed to determine the amount of toll that they had to pay. Other, less vital matters were left to be attended to once the canal opened for business.

Then it was October. The red and yellow leaves were reflected in sparkling water from one end of the Erie Canal to the other. De Witt Clinton had kept his promise, and the state was delirious with happiness. On the splendid autumn morning of October 26, a great celebration got under way to hail the new canal and honor the man who had made it possible.

Another trying problem at Lockport was blasting a channel through solid rock. Cranes (above) were used to lift out the rubble. In the completed cut (below) the tow horses work high above the water.

The festivities started in Buffalo. A parade, led by a brass band, escorted Governor Clinton and other dignitaries from the red-brick courthouse through the town to the canal. There they boarded the *Seneca Chief*, whose bright decorations included a huge oil painting of Clinton depicted as Hercules resting from his labors. On the deck were two colorfully painted kegs. Both held water from Lake Erie. Later, in New York, they were to be poured into the ocean with a mixture of waters from the Mississippi, Columbia, Thames, La Plata, Seine, Rhine, Orinoco, Amazon, Nile, Gambia, Indus, and Ganges rivers in a "Wedding of the Waters." Four other canalboats followed the *Seneca Chief* in the official flotilla. One, *Noah's Ark*, carried two Indian boys, a bear, two young deer, a beaver, two

When all the canal was opened in 1825, packet boats appeared at once. This fall scene is called Late afternoon calm on the Erie.

Harper's Weekly, FEB. 22, 1873

Collector's Office, *Oct 13 1851.*

I, B. Lowell

Master of the Boat *Livingston* of *Rochester*
Do Certify that the following is a full and true statement of the present Cargo of the said Boat, and that I have paid Toll thereon as follows:
To *Mve* for original cargo, on Clearance No. 542
To for additional cargo,

ARTICLES.	WHERE FROM.	WHERE BOUND.	Weight—lbs.	Miles.	Rates.	TOLLS.
Boat	Troy	Buffalo		357	5z	12 50
Mdze	"		29472	"	9	94 69
Castings	"	Rochester	12984	2z	45	15 31
Mdze	"		2342	"	9	5 52
Furniture	"	Jordan	1337	183	45	1 10
		Buffalo	46137			129 12
Add by Scale Mdze			1205			4 19
						133 31

B. Lowell

Among the final projects to be completed on the Erie were the weighlocks. These stations were often elaborate structures, both in New York state (right) and on Pennsylvania's canals (above). A boat entered the lock and was weighed either by a cradlelike scale (below) or by the volume of water it displaced. As the toll bill at left indicates, the canalboat and its several articles of freight were charged according to the weight and the number of miles to be traveled.

The Canals of Pennsylvania, 1901

69

The climax of the 523-mile, nine-day procession which formally opened the entire Erie Canal was the "Wedding of the Waters." In this dramatic ceremony, portrayed in the painting above, Governor Clinton poured one of the two kegs of water from Lake Erie into the Atlantic Ocean just south of the New York harbor. The colorful keg in the photograph at right was one that Clinton emptied.

eagles, various other birds, and even a tank of fish. Its purpose was to symbolize the West before the coming of the white man.

The five boats left Buffalo at 10 A.M. At that moment, a cannon was fired. A few moments later another cannoneer, a number of miles farther down the canal, heard the sound and fired his gun. In this way the message was relayed all the way from Buffalo to New York City, 500 miles away. The last signal, which was fired at 11:20 A.M., then triggered a tremendous artillery salute from New York. Then the line of gunners sent the same signal booming back, to let Buffalo know that New York had received the message.

The boats, each towed by a team of horses, had a quiet trip between towns because most of the country through which the canal ran was still wilderness. But at every town and hamlet there was food and speechmaking. Many communities sent boats to join the official flotilla which soon stretched far along the canal.

Canal towns had been preparing since midsummer for this event. Most of them had constructed what were called transparencies—boxes that had letters cut into their faces with lanterns inside so their message could be read night or day. They were hung everywhere; small ones on the sides of cabins saying merely CLINTON, or great arch-shaped ones like the huge sign spanning the canal at Montezuma that proclaimed DE WITT CLINTON

AND INTERNAL IMPROVEMENTS. Fireworks were shot from the stone-arch aqueduct at Rochester. Tiny Buckville could afford nothing so grand, but did its best by voting to keep every cabin in the village lighted until midnight.

Some of the towns along the canal, however, gave Clinton an icy reception. Rome, for instance, had grown into a thriving town on the canal built by the old Western Inland Lock Navigation Company. But the Erie had bypassed it by nearly half a mile, and prosperous businesses found themselves facing a stagnant ditch. Some of the unhappy citizens held their own "Wedding of the Waters" before Clinton and his fleet arrived. In a funeral-like procession, the townspeople carried a barrel of water from the old canal and dumped it into the Erie.

Schenectady was equally cold. The town had become prosperous by hauling people and freight from the Hudson River to Mohawk River boats. The Erie Canal might be good for the country but it had ruined Schenectady's specialized business, and so the townspeople completely ignored Clinton's arrival. However, the students of Union College in the city, being young and optimistic about the canal, saved the day by warmly welcoming and entertaining the governor and his party.

On November 2, after a trip of about a week, the *Seneca Chief* and her large following passed from the

Erie Canal into the Hudson River. After a celebration that lasted far into the night, the boats headed down the Hudson toward New York City. There, two steamboats were able to pull the entire fleet of canalboats down the Hudson to the harbor.

Governor Clinton was met by cannon salutes from the city's forts, by city dignitaries, and by swarms of boats with tooting whistles and cheer-

ing passengers. The *Seneca Chief* was towed out to Sandy Hook where the New York harbor joins the Atlantic, and the ceremony of the "Wedding of the Waters" was carried out. Clinton poured the two kegs of Lake Erie water into the ocean as a symbol that the Great Lakes and the Atlantic were now united. Then the mixture of river waters was emptied as a sign that commerce from all parts of the world

could now be carried to the American West. Before the brief ceremony had ended, Clinton's face was wet with tears of emotion; he had worked so hard and suffered so much disappointment, and now at last the canal was truly finished.

New York City that day saw one of the greatest celebrations in its history. A parade, which is said to have been five miles long, reached the Battery

Ships of many sizes and several nations took part in the canal-opening pageant (above) in New York harbor. "Never before was there such a fleet collected, and so superbly decorated," wrote one exuberant observer of the gathering, "and it is very possible that a display so grand, so beautiful, and we may add sublime, will never again be witnessed."

just in time to welcome Clinton as he stepped ashore. There were spectacular fireworks, and the city was hung everywhere with transparencies hailing Clinton and the canal. During the evening, crowds walked by City Hall to admire the fairyland sight of a building lighted by thousands of candles. Among the dignitaries in New York for the festivities was President John Quincy Adams. He was accompanied by former Presidents John Adams, Jefferson, Madison, and Monroe, as well as the hotheaded politician Andrew Jackson.

Meanwhile, in the New England states, families held their own quiet little celebrations. Now with smooth water all the way and no need to hire expensive wagon transport, the long journey to the western lands became much easier and cheaper. In New Hampshire and Connecticut, Massachusetts and Vermont, families packed the farm wagons that would carry them on the first leg of the trip. They took a final look at the house and barn and fields that were being abandoned to wind and rain and time— with so many people leaving, no one was buying farms. Then they turned away from the old home and did not look back again. From that moment, everything lay ahead, with the Erie Canal a shining ribbon leading to a new land and a new life.

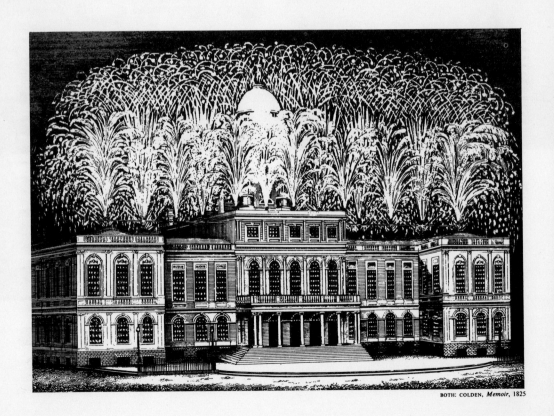

BOTH: COLDEN, *Memoir*, 1825

Capping New York's celebration, fountains of sparks burst forth from the City Hall roof (left). Earlier in the day a parade many miles long honored the Erie and its foremost supporter. A fire company named after Clinton took part in the parade and proudly displayed the poster above. A company engine is seen fancifully pictured against a panorama of the Mohawk Valley with an aqueduct spanning treacherous rapids.

4 TRAVEL ON THE ERIE

From the moment the Erie Canal opened, its waters were thronged with lines of vessels moving in opposite directions. The press of traffic was so great, particularly during the autumn and spring seasons, that boats often had to wait for hours before they could get through the locks. The Erie was too small for the amount of business it carried the very day that De Witt Clinton's triumph was proclaimed.

The nation had never seen anything like it. The major east–west transport of goods and people moved along the Erie, and each year the traffic increased. There was a constant bustle of emigrants going west to find new homes; of European visitors coming to see the sights they had read about; of politicians, merchants, army officers, and cattle traders; of clergymen trying to save souls, and gamblers busily separating careless travelers from their money. Cargo boats moving toward Lake Erie carried clocks, guns, needles, knives, whalebone corsets, bolts of cloth, and a thousand other articles the West wanted. Boats from the West carried the produce of farm and forest to the cities of the East Coast: potatoes, apples, cider, wheat and milled flour, whiskey, live

A crowded packet rounds a bend on the canal. From its opening days the Erie was jammed with traffic—the eastbound boats deep laden with freight, and the westbound boats top-heavy with passengers.

turkeys, lumber, and precious furs.

Life was exciting for the people who traveled on Erie water, or worked on the canal, or lived beside it. Canal towns grew as fast as houses, mills, and stores could be built by overworked carpenters and masons. Even the smallest hamlets shared in the excitement of the canal; timorous indeed was the Erie businessman who did not put up a canalside grocery, a grogshop, or perhaps a livery stable. But even for folks who just watched the boats go by, the Big Ditch always provided something of interest.

In 1826, the canal was kept open from late February through early December—its first full season. During that period thousands of boats were entering the canal through the eastern terminus, and it was quite common for as many as fifty boats to set out in a single day. In the following years, traffic on the Erie became even heavier than that. As for the tolls collected that first year, they were almost too good to be believed. The Erie and Champlain canals took in $762,000 or about one-tenth the cost of building the two waterways. Even the greatest optimists had expected nothing like this.

Besides the long-haul boats, a multitude of local craft cluttered the waterway. These boats had been built by men bitten by canal fever, and their creations were often strangely shaped and weirdly colored. The Erie also took care of a large amount of traffic from branch canals leading from Lake Ontario, and Seneca and Cayuga lakes. Rafts brought produce from hundreds of farms along these waterways to join eastbound shipping on the Erie Canal.

Westbound traffic was dominated by numberless emigrants. Some of them spoke with New England twangs, and others in all the accents of western Europe. But the talk was always the same: land prices in Illinois or Indiana or Ohio; and how many bushels of corn an acre of the fertile prairie land could grow.

There were many songs popular on the canal in those years; and one, though it deserves no fame for the quality of its verse, truly caught the spirit of the times:

Then there's old Vermont; well, what
    do you think of that?
To be sure the gals are handsome and
    the cattle very fat.
But who among the mountains, amid
    the cloud and snow
    would stay,
When he can buy a prairie in
    Michigan-eye-ay.
Yea, yea, yea, in Michigan-eye-ay.
Then there's the state of New York
    where some are very rich,
Themselves and a few others have dug
    a mighty Ditch
To render it more easy for us to find
    the way,
And sail upon the waters to
    Michigan-eye-ay.
Yea, yea, yea, to Michigan-eye-ay.

There was a wide variety of craft

The Erie served as a route to the vast unsettled spaces of inland
America for European immigrants as well as for eastern Americans.
Above, a shipload of Irish immigrants arrives in New York in 1847.
Below, another group of brawny European workers is herded ashore
there. Many would later travel farther west on Erie Canal boats.

Above, freight barges are taking on cargo in New York. From there
a Hudson steamer will tow ten or so at a time upriver to the Erie.

A warning that was heard often on Erie boats inspired the writing of this song. It was one of a great many ballads about the canal.

on the canal, but the packet boat was queen of the Erie water. She topped all other boats in both speed and luxury. A packet used the best horses and changed them often; she sometimes traveled day and night, and always had the right of way. All other craft had to move aside when a packet boat's steersman shouted out a passing warning to their crews. Since there was usually a towpath on only one side of the canal, the boat being passed would have to relax its towlines and move over toward the opposite bank. The packet would then pass over these lines and continue on her way.

During the day packet travel often provided pleasure and excitement. There was much to watch as the boat glided past forested areas, small villages, and through growing cities. Passengers could take their ease on a bench on the roof of the cabin; or when waiting at the locks or if traffic became tiresome, they could always jump ashore and go for a short walk on the towpath. One of the most common ways of getting back aboard a canalboat was to wait on one of the low bridges that crossed the canal and then drop onto the cabin as the boat passed beneath.

Those same bridges, however, made it impossible for a passenger to fall into complete dreamy relaxation as he rode. The canal crews had built more than 300 "occupation bridges" for divided farms and interrupted roads. Even more were being built as the country along the canal became settled. Since it was cheaper, the bridges were built low, but this also made them hazardous for travelers. As a boat moved along, the warning cry came at regular intervals from the steersman, "Low bridge! Everybody down!" Anyone who failed to bend or crouch down near the deck was knocked down or swept overboard, and often seriously injured.

Passengers were fed three tremendous meals a day. A typical menu included several kinds of meat, fowl, and fish, as well as potatoes, two or three kinds of bread, various vegetables and pickles, a choice of pies and cakes, and of course, coffee and tea. When fares were first established, they were set at four cents a mile for through passengers, meals included. It took no time at all for the sharp-

The low bridges so hazardous to canalboat passengers were a boon to those trying to get back aboard. They would simply drop onto the deck as the boat passed beneath.

witted to discover that they could go aboard a packet as passengers just at mealtime, stuff themselves with a huge meal, and then step ashore a half hour or so later after paying a fare of only a few pennies. It was all perfectly legal, but the fares were changed after a howl went up from most of the canalboat captains.

For packets running around the clock, fresh teams of horses, stabled along the way in line barns, were changed regularly. The speed limit on the canal was four miles an hour, to prevent the wash from swift-moving boats from wearing away the banks. However, packet captains often speeded up their teams to six or seven miles an hour to gain time. Of course, by speeding, the captain was breaking the law and was liable for a fine of ten dollars; but he could earn a great

When the sun was out and the weather warm, a packet's deck was an ideal spot to sit and watch the countryside pass slowly by, as the ladies and gentlemen in this painting are doing. The canal here is the Delaware and Hudson, which was opened four years after the Erie.

deal more than that by making good time. He would merely jump ashore at the toll collector's office, throw down his ten dollars, and keep right on going.

Some captains were indeed high-handed. There are many tall tales of illegal races on the canal. As two packets came to a lock one boat would try to pass, and the other to stay in the lead. Then, as the stories

A NEW BERTH.

Candid Landlady. "THE FIRST FROM THE TOP, SIR, IS THE ONLY BED VACANT; BUT YOU HAVE GOT VERY NICE NEIGHBORS—ONE GENTLEMAN CHEWS, BUT THE OTHERS ONLY SMOKE!"

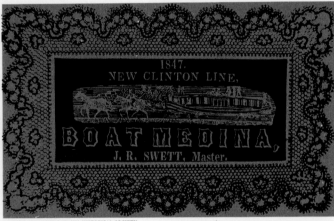

1847.
NEW CLINTON LINE,
BOAT MEDINA,
J. R. SWETT, Master.

A packet ticket (center) was usually good for a multi-tiered packet berth. The cramped bunks were the object of much Erie Canal humor, including the magazine cartoon above. In the drawing below, a top-berth passenger climbs to his perch as other gentlemen wait for the captain to call their names from the bed list. The ladies' bedroom is separated by the curtain at the rear.

went, tempers would run high, insults fly back and forth, and one crew would violate all the rules of fair play and cut the other's line. Life on the canal could be rough.

At night, the cabin became the sleeping quarters. Narrow bunks were put up along the walls where they were stacked two- and sometimes three-high. The forward part of the cabin was the ladies' section, and on the more elegant boats, a curtain was drawn across at night to separate it from the men's section. Otherwise the men remained on deck until the ladies turned in, before descending to their own bunks.

The British writer Charles Dickens made a trip on a packet and described the way the cabin was transformed into sleeping quarters when night fell. "Going below, I found suspended on either side of the cabin, three long tiers of hanging bookshelves, designed apparently for volumes of the small octavo size. Looking with great attention at these contrivances (wondering to find such literary preparations in such a place) I descried on each shelf a sort of microscopic sheet and blanket; then I began to dimly comprehend that the passengers were the library, and that they were to be arranged edgewise on these shelves, till morning."

Mayor Philip Hone of New York City was not reminded of anything so pleasant as a library; he remarked that the sleepers were "packed away like dead pigs in a Cincinnati pork warehouse." With so many travelers clamoring for places, the packets were usually crowded far beyond what they had been built to carry. One British tourist reported that, "Mattresses completely covered the floor, on which people lay as close as possible. The dinner table was covered with sleeping humanity, more thickly than Captain Davis ever strewed it with beefsteaks, and those who lay under the table thought themselves favored, inasmuch as they could not be trodden upon."

The bunks were simply frames with canvas tacked over them, attached to the wall on one side but supported on the outside by chains or leather straps from the ceiling. The supports sometimes gave way and there was much merriment in the room as two or even three men were tumbled to the floor. There was absolutely no privacy. A person had to edge into his narrow berth with everyone watching. Of course under such conditions, there was little undressing for bed; most people took off no more than shoes, and perhaps a coat. Once in his bunk, the would-be sleeper found it too narrow and too close to the one above to allow him to turn over during the night. Then the boots of crewmen clumping overhead on the cabin roof, the symphony of snores and squalling children, and the assorted sounds of the busy canalside made the night something to be painfully endured by all but the most hardy.

Some of the experiences of this

Boatmen and passengers visit or do chores while waiting to pass through the locks at West Troy where the Champlain and Erie canals joined. This peaceful scene was painted by John Hill around 1835.

kind of luxury travel were humorous —at least to a person looking back on them. Frederick Gerstaecker, a German traveler, wrote about his night on a packet: "I awoke with a dreadful feeling of suffocation; cold perspiration stood on my forehead and I could hardly draw my breath; there was a weight like lead on my stomach and chest. I attempted to cry out—in vain; I lay almost without consciousness. The weight remained immovable; above me was a noise like distant thunder. It was my companion of the upper story, who lay snoring over my head; and that the weight which pressed on my chest was caused by his body no longer remained a doubtful point. I endeavored to move the Colossus—impossible. I tried to push, to cry out—in vain. He lay like a rock on my chest and seemed to have no more feeling."

In his plight, Gerstaecker just managed to reach his cravat pin and jab sharply right where the weight was heaviest. There was a cry of "What's that? Murder! Help!" from above. Then the weight was momentarily lifted and Gerstaecker slid out and stood on the floor. In the dim lamplight he discovered that the worn canvas of the bunk above had ripped under the weight of his fat neighbor, and that the man, in effect, had been sitting on Gerstaecker's chest. The pin thrust had caused the man to jerk upward, allowing Gerstaecker to escape. But now the canvas had split even more, so that the unfortunate man was sitting on the bunk below with his head and feet still in his own, crying, half-asleep, "Help! Murder!"

However, most accounts of packet travel indicate that it was a more comfortable way to travel than roads: in that period it was the fastest, and by far the smoothest. Yet, packets could carry only the hand luggage of passengers and so were not useful to emigrant families going west to settle. A family with livestock, household goods, and other possessions usually traveled on a lineboat—a freight boat which allowed settlers to set up camp and cookstoves on deck. A lineboat's deck was a busy place indeed. There were children swarming over and around the various piles of belongings, while smoke rose from an

Among the many kinds of craft that cruised the Erie Canal were the cargo-carrying lakers pictured above. These blunt-nosed barges are seen tied up in the canalboat basin at Oswego. The sketch at left shows a bullhead, a canalboat very closely related to the laker. The two differed mainly in the arrangement of decks and cabins.

Many men and beasts spent nearly all the days and nights of their lives on the Erie. The overworked horses of the lineboats stayed on board (left) when they were not towing or debarking to eat grass (below). The barge families made the best of the boats' cramped cabins (above, right). For the cooking (right) and washing there was always plenty of fresh water at hand, and usually a good drying breeze as the clothesline (below, right) moved slowly down the canal.

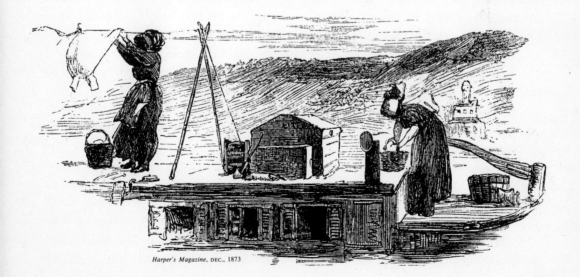

Harper's Magazine, DEC., 1873

93

The canal soon became as commonplace as a main street; at times
hardly anyone noticed a boat cruising through a canalside town.

assortment of stoves as women pre-
pared meals for their families.

There was little luxury on a lineboat. Sleeping on stacks of possessions was probably as comfortable as
the cramped, stuffy quarters of the
packets, but the pleasures of being in
the fresh air turned sour when an all-
day rain was falling. A lineboat was
considerably slower than a packet and
often ran only during daylight. These
lineboats were operated by companies,
and the quality of the equipment and
teams used on them depended on how
much money they were making from
the business. This meant that, with
old horses frequently changed, the
lineboat could make little more than

fifty to sixty miles in a good day. But
a packet boat could cover about eighty
miles in twenty-four hours.

The life of the captain of a lineboat
was not an easy one. He needed vigi-
lance to beat out competitors for
freight; he needed stamina; and he
often needed a clever pair of fists to
help him settle disputes with other
captains. The boats were the only
homes many captains knew. Their
wives cooked and kept house in the
tiny cabins. They hung out washing on
lines on deck which were set low to
prevent disasters at low bridges. Children were raised on board, and even
the tow horses were part of the family.
When the horses were not working

A canalboat family posed for this photograph while mother held the tiller, and her children sat atop the boat's feeding brace of mules.

they were brought on board and kept in stalls.

Timber rafts were a type of craft particularly detested by all other boatmen on the canal. Long and clumsy, they were drawn by oxen which could go no faster than a mile and a half an hour. A timber raft could be several hundred feet long, and was made up of as many as ten sections of logs, called cribs, hitched together. The cribs had to be uncoupled at locks so they could pass through one at a time. Canal regulations stated that other boats could take their turn with the cribs going through a lock, but it did nothing to make the rafters more popular.

There were many other kinds of craft on the waterway. Shanty boats, moored where the canal was broadest, were little more than shacks on rafts, but to their owners they were home. Entire families lived out their lives and died on the Erie. There were also floating shops of tinkers and menders, traveling sellers of potions and liniments, water-borne penny museums, and a hundred other enterprises drifting from village to village.

There was freight to be moved west and produce to be shipped east. There were small fortunes to be made, land to be bought and sold, and a whole new country to be settled. All this was made possible by the Erie Canal.

95

5 THE CANAL CRAZE

The Erie was not even finished before canals were being dug or plans drawn up for canals in half a dozen other states. Some were sensible, modest waterways, designed to help farmers get their produce to market, and to help miners and millers reach the seaboard with their products. But far too many canals were built on dreams, and they were often just about as solid.

The success of the Erie had made everyone canal-crazy. Those men who had said that the Erie would never pay its own way were now predicting success for every half-hatched plan to build a canal that came their way. The clink of money dropping into the toll collectors' boxes up in New York made a sound that interfered with good, straight thinking. No one stopped to consider that the Erie was prosperous because it lay in the only passage through the Appalachian wall; no other canal could possibly have such a clear advantage.

Actually, only a few canal systems were built to compete directly with the Erie for a share in the tremendous Western market. Only one of these actually made it across the mountains—the Pennsylvania system,

*America's most complex boat route was the Pennsylvania system. Its
Portage Railroad (below) hauled boats over the Allegheny Mountains.
The rail cars were originally drawn by horses on the level stretches.*

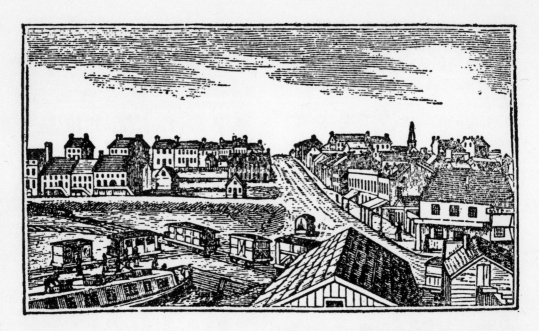

Railroads were the only practical way some ambitious canal planners could overcome
hills and valleys far steeper
than any the Erie had to con-
tend with. Above, passengers
transfer from a packet on a
canal portion of the Pennsylvania Mainline to board
the Portage Railroad at Hollidaysburg for the trip over
the Alleghenies. At right
is one of the twenty-three
portage rail sections on
New Jersey's Morris Canal.

or the Mainline as it was then called. It was the most complicated of them all: a weird combination of waterways, horse-drawn railways, and cable cars.

Philadelphia, like Boston and Baltimore, had not been overjoyed by the success of the Erie Canal. New York City had been outstripping them all in commerce and growth since 1807, and the Erie made New York even more prosperous. Philadelphia decided to build a canal, like the Erie, which would bring lucrative trade back to the city and the state. What difference if there was no break in Pennsylvania's western mountains? Put it over them! With this spirit the canal system became one of the engineering marvels of its day—but it was so complicated that it could never pay for itself. Construction on the Pennsylvania system started with the usual hurrahs, fireworks, and spadefuls of earth on July 4, 1826. (Ever since the groundbreaking ceremony on the Erie on July 4, 1817, it had become almost an unwritten law that canal building should start on Independence Day.) From that day the new canal went ahead full speed. The engineers made use of the experience gained on the Erie since many of them had learned their business on the Big Ditch. But they could not overcome the geographic fact that Pennsylvania was not a good place to build a canal to the West.

When the various parts of the canal's main route were finished in 1834,

The canal craze created shipping patchworks like the one advertised in this old poster. Goods moving from New York to Boston traveled by steamboat, canalboat, and railroad.

a traveler got quite a ride for his money. The system, running on land and water and almost in the air from Philadelphia to Pittsburgh, became known as the Grand Canal. Leaving from Philadelphia on the first leg of the journey, a passenger traveled on a conveyance called the State Railroad. This consisted of coaches with railroad-car wheels which were pulled by horses to the foot of a long, high hill. The horses were unhitched and the coaches were then drawn to the top by a powerful cable. At the summit two or three coaches were coupled together, new horses hitched on, and they were off, on this oddest of canals, to Columbia, about seventy-five miles away. There, at last, the traveler boarded a boat. From Columbia, a true canal ran 173 miles beside the Susquehanna and Juniata rivers through 111 locks, as far as Hollidaysburg. At that town the waterway ended and an even more peculiar part of the trip began.

As the crow flies, Hollidaysburg is only thirty-five miles from Johnstown, but between the two lies the crest of the Allegheny Mountains. To reach one town from the other, one must travel up and down almost 2,600 feet. By comparison, the Erie had ups and downs totaling only 688 feet in 363 miles. A canal between the two points could only have been a huge series of locks, and it would have taken a couple of days to get a boat through. The engineers met the challenge by building another "railroad" over the

mountains. This one, finished in 1828, was called the Portage Railroad, and it was another of the many canal-inspired engineering triumphs.

Passengers got into cars whose wheels rolled on wooden rails capped by iron bars; they were then pulled up the slopes by great ropes (later wire cables) drawn by engines above. There were five separate slopes, or inclined planes, carved in the mountain on either side of the summit, with level stretches of several miles between the top of each slope and the bottom of the next. After a car had been drawn up one inclined plane by motorized cable, horses pulled it to the bottom of the next. At the summit there was a hotel where travelers could spend the night before starting down the other side. All this made for a great deal of hitching and unhitching. Even in its most efficient period, the Portage Railroad required thirty-three power changes.

The railroad ended at Johnstown, on the western side of the mountains. There the traveler boarded a canal packet once more for the trip to Pittsburgh where the Grand Canal ended at the Ohio River. On the Ohio, steamboats and flatboats headed straight into the promised land. The trip from Philadelphia to Pittsburgh was 394 miles, and required four full days. It included two railroads and two separate canal sections with 177 locks, almost twice as many as the Erie. The builders originally planned to extend the canal from Pittsburgh to

The Lemon House (above) was a famous inn and station house on the Allegheny Portage Railroad. Here passengers are shown leaving the inn to board a waiting train.

The old stone sleepers of the Portage Railroad can still be seen in the hills between Hollidaysburg and Johnstown. These rail supports, photographed at left, were used instead of wooden crossties on many early American lines.

PIONEER
FAST LINE,

BY RAIL ROAD CARS AND CANAL PACKETS

From Philadelphia to Pittsburgh,

THROUGH IN 3½ DAYS:

AND BY STEAM BOATS, CARRYING THE UNITED STATES' MAIL.

From PITTSBURGH to LOUISVILLE.

Starts every morning, from the corner of Broad & Race St.

In large and splendid eight wheel cars, vin the *Lancaster and Harrisburg Rail Roads*, arriving at the latter place, at 4 o'clock, in the afternoon. where passengers will take the Packets, which have all been fitted up in a very superior manner, having been built *expressly for the accommodation of Passengers*, after the most approved models of Boats used on the Erie Canal, and are not surpassed by the Boats used upon any other Line.

The Boats are commanded by old and experienced Captains, several of whom have been connected with the Line for the two last seasons. For speed and comfort, this Line is not excelled by any other in the United States.

Passengers for Cincinnati, Louisville, Natchez, Nashville, St. Louis, &c.

Will always be certain of being taken on without delay, as this Line connects with the Boats at Pittsburgh, carrying the Mail.

OFFICE, N. E. CORNER OF FOURTH AND CHESNUT ST.

For seats apply as above; and at No. 200 Market Street; at the White Swan Hotel, Race Street; at the N. E. corner of Third and Willow Street; No. 31 South Third Street; and at the West Chester House, Broad Street.

Philadelphia, April, 1837

A. B. CUMMINGS, Agent.

Young, Printer, Black Horse Alley, Philadelphia

Special sectional packets were eventually used on the Pennsylvania system so that passengers would not have to change carriers. The rear half of such a boat is about to leave Philadelphia (above). After a train ride, it joined its front half for a canal trip and then both rode the Portage Railroad (below). As the poster at left shows, earlier travelers had to transfer to train cars to make the portage.

103

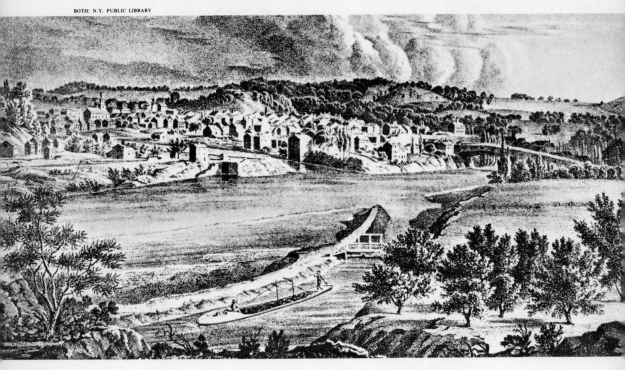

Easton, Pennsylvania, was the junction for several canals. In the foreground of the drawing above, a boat has just passed through the lock between the Morris Canal and the Delaware River at Easton.

Lake Erie, but they were so discouraged by mounting costs and the difficulties facing them in the remaining miles, that they never pushed construction beyond Pittsburgh.

The Portage Railroad became something that all visitors to the United States wanted to see. Charles Dickens, who had been so amused by sleeping arrangements on an Erie Canal packet, was very much impressed by his trip on the railroad: "Occasionally the rails were laid on the extreme verge of a giddy precipice; and looking from the carriage window, the traveler gazes sheer down, without a stone or scrap of fence between, into the mountain depths below. . . . It was very pretty traveling thus at a rapid pace along the heights of the mountains in a keen wind, to look down into a valley full of light and softness, catching glimpses, through the trees, of scattered cabins . . . men in their shirt sleeves, looking on at their unfinished houses, planning out tomorrow's work, and we riding onward, high above them like a whirlwind."

The Grand Canal was completely opened in 1834, nine years after the Erie. Like New York state, Pennsylvania later went on to add branches

104

The Eastern Division of the Pennsylvania Canal—so called to distinguish it from the section of the canal that ran west of the Alleghenies—is seen here about 1835, alongside the Susquehanna River.

to the canal system. The handicap of having to transfer passengers and freight from one carrier to another was later partially overcome by building sectional canalboats. The sections, with freight and passengers aboard, were loaded onto railroad cars at Philadelphia and hauled to Columbia. There they were put in the canal and fastened together to form a canalboat for the trip to the Portage Railroad. At the railroad the boat was uncoupled again, the sections hauled over the tracks, and coupled once more for the trip by water to Pittsburgh.

The Pennsylvania canal system with its specially built boats, its numerous locks, and its two railroads was both slow and expensive. It never paid its way and ran the state deeply into debt. Yet, contemporary accounts claim that during its peak, the system was so crowded day and night, that at least forty boats carrying westbound freight and travelers could be counted at any place along the Grand Canal.

On July 4, 1828, President John Quincy Adams delivered his speech and thrust a spade into the earth on the banks of the Potomac River just above Washington. He struck a root, tried again, and hit another. Then he took off his coat, grasped the spade firmly, and on his third try, thrust it deep and turned over a good shovelful of earth. This delighted the cheering crowd. The ceremony marked the challenge of Virginia and Maryland to the Erie Canal for a share in the commerce with the West. This was a new beginning for the Potomac Company first organized in 1785 to dig a similar canal. The company ran out of money before it could finish the proposed waterway, but it did manage to build twelve locks. Many of these were in good condition when the company was reorganized in 1825 to build the Chesapeake and Ohio Canal. It was to run beside the Potomac to Cumberland, Maryland, and then cross the mountains to the Youghiogheny River, a tributary of

the Ohio, which offered a direct avenue to the West.

The city of Baltimore wanted to get in on the great project, and immediately made plans to dig a branch canal from the city to join the main waterway. But that idea was quickly dropped when a brief survey showed that the great number of locks needed to climb over the hills would make the branch far too costly. It was decided, instead, to build a railroad. So, on the same day President Adams was having so much trouble with the roots, another ceremony was being held in Baltimore to launch the first horse-drawn segment of the Baltimore and Ohio Railroad.

The C & O Canal progressed slowly. Sickness plagued the workers. The Irish and German immigrant work crews disliked each other so bitterly

Maryland's answer to the Erie, the Chesapeake and Ohio, required seventy-five locks, including the one at left. The photographs above show an aqueduct and another lock on the C & O about 1900.

Constructed primarily to carry coal from the Lackawanna region of New York and Pennsylvania, the Delaware and Hudson Canal is probably the waterway seen in this 1899 painting of a packet at a lock.

that they had to be kept apart to prevent fights. And even Irishmen from different counties in the old country engaged in monumental battles, helped along by plentiful supplies of cheap whiskey. Construction was often difficult, and at one point a tunnel more than half a mile long had to be dug.

Legal troubles with the Baltimore and Ohio Railroad also slowed progress on the canal. When the railroad reached the Potomac, the company decided to keep on laying track, and continued to run alongside the canal. At one place there was a narrow pass wide enough for only one of them. A long court battle ensued, but the canal emerged victorious. Not to be stopped, the railroad tunneled through the rock and again continued along beside the canal. By that time the railroad had long since changed its horses for steam engines.

The Chesapeake and Ohio Canal got as far as Cumberland, Maryland, where it was to have started over the mountain crest—but there it stopped. The completed portion was 185 miles long, and had cost over $11,000,000, far more than anyone had thought possible. And that was the end of one more dream, although the canal continued to carry freight, especially coal, long after many other waterways had fallen into disuse.

The canal frenzy even reached out to the new states on the western side of the mountains. Ohio, Indiana, and Illinois had all gained statehood by

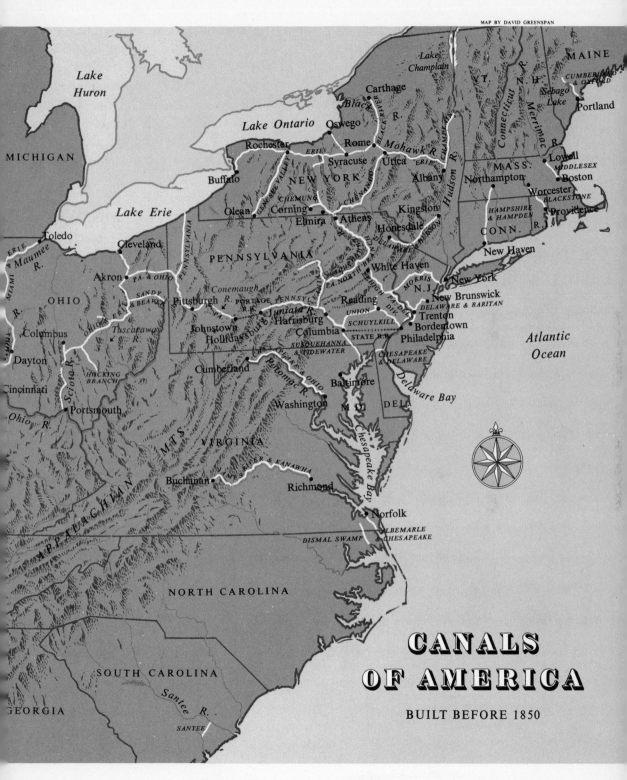

CANALS OF AMERICA

BUILT BEFORE 1850

Following the Erie's lead, the American canals reached far into the West by 1850. Most of them are shown here, marked in white.

1818, but seven years later they were still sparsely settled and woefully underdeveloped. News of the Erie Canal struck a happy note on the frontier. At that time, road builders were not able to construct highways that would bear up under bad weather and heavy use, so rivers remained the only efficient means for hauling goods and passengers. The frontier states decided that the best way to bring settlers and commerce to the wilderness was to build their own canals as quickly as possible.

De Witt Clinton took time off from work on the Erie to break ground for a canal system in Ohio on July 4, 1825. The state had an extremely ambitious and complicated plan: It consisted of two main canals running generally north to south the length of the state, from Lake Erie to the Ohio River. Clinton broke ground first for the easternmost of the two, called the Ohio and Erie Canal. Then he journeyed clear across the state to launch the other waterway—the Miami and Erie Canal.

Work on the two canals continued for eight years. Sickness again was a greater obstacle than engineering problems, for clouds of malaria-carrying mosquitoes swarmed in swamps and bogs. It was believed then that whiskey helped ward off the combination of fever and chills, and every crew had a man who came around every few hours to hand out shots of

Harper's Magazine, SEPT., 1856

Harper's Weekly, APRIL 26, 1884

The Dismal Swamp Canal was completed in 1829. The painting of it above shows a famous inn that stood where the canal crossed from Virginia into North Carolina. But the sail and steam-driven vessels were imaginary—most of the canal's traffic consisted of barges carrying wood from small lumbering operations in the swamp (far left). For this canal, workers had to build dikes and dig ditches to cope with the waterlogged soil. At left, men are constructing a drainage ditch to reclaim farmland from the swamp.

the strong remedy to the diggers.

The Ohio canals soon generated their own De Witt Clinton, a man named Alfred Kelley. Like Clinton, Kelley kept pushing construction year after year in spite of engineering problems, money shortages, sickness that laid his workers out, constant exposure to weather, and often personal danger. He grew so weary toward the end of construction that the state legislature ordered him to take a vacation, but he paid no attention to them. Finally, his weakened health forced him to conduct all business from bed. It appeared that

only a miracle could keep him alive to see the completion of his canals— but years later Alfred Kelley was still an active politician.

The Ohio canals were largely finished by 1832, although the Miami and Erie did not reach the lake until 1845. The Ohio and Erie Canal was 309 miles long and had 152 locks and 14 aqueducts. The Miami and Erie Canal ran for 244 miles and had 105 locks and 22 aqueducts. Like most canals of the period, they never paid for themselves. But they did open up commerce for Ohio farms and villages, and enabled them to buy from

NEW-YORK HISTORICAL SOCIETY

Schemes for waterways west, long cherished by Southerners such as Washington and Jefferson, were partly realized by two canals that ran beside major southern rivers. The Chesapeake and Ohio skirted the Potomac, avoiding its unnavigable rapids (above). The James River and Kanawha Canal (right) paralleled Virginia's James River.

114

and sell to the rest of the country. Thanks in great part to her hundreds of miles of commercial waterways, Ohio became the third most populous state in the Union before the canal era ended.

Indiana was even less developed than Ohio. Except for the older settlements along the Ohio River, the state consisted of little more than a few handfuls of settlers trying to carve cornfields out of hardwood forests. The Hoosiers were bitten by the canal bug as early as their Ohio neighbors; but there were so few of them and the job was so big, that all they could do

for several years was discuss routes. Finally, in 1832, they decided to connect the upper Wabash River with Ohio's Miami and Erie Canal in order to reach Lake Erie.

This project was not spared the plague of disease either. It was said that over one stretch of canal a worker died for every six feet of completed channel. Cemeteries were closed when they contained a thousand bodies, and new ones were started. Recruiters were busy in the East luring new workers with offers of two dollars and roast beef every day. This kept them coming although too few lived

long enough to enjoy many paydays.

When the first section of the canal was opened, the Hoosiers were so enthusiastic over their waterway in the wilderness, that the legislature voted to extend it farther south along the Wabash. A year later, the representatives went completely wild and voted to add still more miles, with a big loop down to the central part of the state. Before it was all over, they had lengthened it once more, all the way to Evansville on the Ohio River. That made it 397 miles long—one of the longest canals built in America. The channel, however, did not reach the Ohio until 1851, and by then railroads were beginning to steal away much of its business.

The Wabash and Erie Canal was open its entire length only a few years: It was a colossal financial failure. The tolls were never even enough to keep it in repair, and the state bore the crushing burden of a $17,000,000 debt. But in another way it was very successful: It brought people into Indiana and through Indiana to settle

Dayton (left) and Cincinnati were connected to Lake Erie and the Eastern markets by the Miami and Erie Canal. The lock below is on a branch canal leading from Columbus to Ohio's second great waterway, the Ohio and Erie.

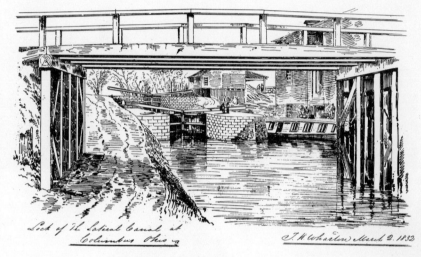

Lock of the Lateral Canal at Columbus Ohio

T. K. Wharton March 2. 1832

territories farther west. As a result, the Wabash and Erie Canal was even more important to the development of the West than the Ohio waterways.

Surprisingly, these backwoods canalmen ran some of the fanciest packet boats in America. Some of the boats boasted furnishings imported from Europe, but Indiana boots, mud, and tobacco juice must have been hard on Brussels carpets. The most famous of the Indiana packets was the *Silver Bell*, which was painted all in silver and was drawn by silver-grey mules whose harnesses sported silver rings and silver bells. Another packet, the *Indiana*, achieved some fame because she had a couple of Hoosier enthusiasts who were always on hand night or day to greet her in Fort Wayne. When they heard she was coming they would drop whatever they were doing, rush to the canal, and play a concert on fiddle and clarinet. At the same time, it was typical of Indiana and the American West that very few boats provided either food or beds for passengers. Frontier hospitality took care

117

Remains of once-active canals may be seen in these photographs. Above are some of the 108 locks on the Black River Canal. At left, a road which was once a towpath runs beside Indiana's Central Canal, below, an old Central aqueduct.

of that problem. When the boat moored for the night the passengers were expected to knock at a settler's door to obtain food and lodging for the night.

The canal-building urge reached its westernmost limit with a waterway leading into the swampy village of Chicago. That canal, called the Illinois and Michigan, was built quite late, between 1836 and 1848. However, the fact that railroads as well as the canal were being constructed through the town caused a wild boom in real estate which sent prices up to fantastic levels.

Chicago's canal connected Lake Michigan with the Illinois River, which flows into the Mississippi. Only a slight height of land separates the two, and it was no great problem to build the canal as far as LaSalle cn the Illinois. There the canalboats met river steamboats. This waterway was surprisingly successful from the start. It never did much business as a packet canal, carrying only occasional picnic parties and annual Sunday school outings; but it was a busy freight handler. In 1848, sugar and other articles reached Buffalo from New Orleans by way of the Illinois and Michigan Canal nearly two weeks before the first canalboat of the season reached Buffalo on the Erie.

Fifteen years after the Erie's opening, there were more than 4,000 miles of canal in the United States. Most of the waterways had been started by optimistic men who were certain that the merry sound of coins being paid for tolls on the Erie would be echoed on their own canals. It seldom worked out that way. The states which were stricken with canal-building fever ended up with a total debt of some $60,000,000—a frightening amount for that time.

Still, canal fever kept running high in New York. Even before the canal was finished, the politicians became convinced that Erie revenue could be stretched to build any number of additional canals. Many rural representatives demanded branch canals for their constituents, and the legislature saw fit to approve several that were not only difficult, but costly and impractical as well. The Black River Canal running north from Rome required 108 locks to carry it up and down a total of 1,081 feet in only thirty-five miles; it took nineteen years to build.

The canal era began with the Erie, and lasted until mid-century. Some of the channels continued in use after that time. But none of them achieved even a faint shadow of the success of the Erie Canal. There was only one Big Ditch.

Yet, all the canals were part of an important period in the growth and settlement of the country, when the West lay empty. They were a way of moving men and goods to the frontier when the growing United States most needed to strengthen her commerce and develop the promise of her bountiful territory.

119

6 THE CANAWLERS

The canals created their own world, and developed their own breed of men. As a matter of fact, they were not even called canals; everyone who worked or lived on them pronounced the word "canawls." Some scholars say that it was the Irish work crews who first started saying it that way, others that it was the Dutch in upper New York state who twisted the sound in that fashion. In any event, it was a canawl, whether it was Erie water or a stretch of channel in sun-bonnet-and-sycamore country out in Indiana.

It took a great many people to run a canal. It was estimated that in 1845 there were 4,000 boats on the Erie with 25,000 men, boys, and women working on them. Then there was a large force of locktenders, towpath walkers who constantly patrolled the canal to watch for the first signs of a leak or break, and repair and maintenance crews. There was a tremendous number of people who did not work directly on the canal but whose canalside shops and services took care of those who traveled or worked on it. And finally, there was a very mixed assortment of those who were there because the canal offered such a rich

120

A boat loads up at a canalside store in Schenectady. The Erie opened new opportunities to New York merchants—and they were grateful. This merchant has proudly hung an Erie Canal mural on his store.

field for their operations: gamblers, thieves, exhibitors of dancing bears, fortune tellers, and the like. A canal was a busy and exciting place to be.

The crew of a canalboat, not counting the captain, numbered anywhere from two to six men. A company-owned packet running day and night might have two steersmen, a cook, probably a general deck hand, and a driver who was changed with his team every fifteen or twenty miles. On a small, owner-run boat there would be only the driver and a steersman; the captain would change off with the steersman and take care of a great many other chores.

A canalboat was steered by a very large rudder which the steersman moved with a long, heavy tiller. A steersman had to be skillful, for his vessel was clumsy and there were an amazing number of things it could run into—other boats, the sides of locks and the canal, and bridge abutments. His importance is shown by his wages which averaged twenty dollars a month with room and board —very good pay on the Erie Canal.

Being a steersman could be quite dangerous. There was a type of boat named the bullhead which was much disliked by steersmen. The bullhead was a cantankerous vessel: except for the bow and stern decks, there was little walking space around the outside of the boat. Nor was there deck space between the front and rear cabins. If a person was anywhere but fore or aft when passing under a low bridge, the only place to go was overboard. There was a ballad about a man who took a job on a bullhead boat and promptly got knocked overboard. It ends like this:

So canawlers take my warning,
    Never steer a bullhead boat,
Or they'll find you some fine morning
    In the E-RI-E afloat.

On quiet stretches of canal, the steersman could daydream, but in busy sections he had to be alert to avoid accidents.

Harper's Magazine, SEPT. 1873

122

The steersman on the Buffalo-based boat above steers outside a west-bound freight boat while the bowman keeps the towline from fouling.

Do all your fine navigating,
  In the line barn full of hay,
And the low bridge you won't be
    hating,
And you'll live to judgment day.

The man, or boy, who drove the tow team was called a hoggee, an old Scottish word for a laborer. He had two or three horses or mules hitched tandem—one ahead of the other—and generally rode on the rear horse. But walking or riding, the job was no picnic. A hoggee usually worked two six-hour shifts a day on the towpath, regardless of cold, rain, or sleet. In his off hours he had to feed and water his team, rub them down, treat chafed places and sores from rubbing collars, and repair harnesses. If there was any time left, he curled up in his clothes and slept.

A hoggee's hours on the towpath also involved more than just keeping

123

the team pulling. On the busy canal, boats were constantly passing and overtaking each other. A daydreaming hoggee could get towlines tangled so quickly that his team might be dragged into the canal. When two boats traveling in opposite directions had to pass each other, the steersman of the outside boat moved to the far side of the canal (or away from the towpath). The hoggee then had to draw his horses to the outside of the towpath and stop them. This allowed his line to go slack so that it lay on the bottom of the towpath and the canal. And then the inside boat, with its horses pulling and its line taut, would cross over the other towline and both boats would continue on their way.

In spite of all the skill and responsibility involved in a driver's work, most of the hoggees were boys barely into their teens. Boys were popular with captains because they were cheaper (twelve dollars a month for men drivers and ten dollars for a boy was the common wage), and they were easier to bully and cheat. Some captains deliberately mistreated their young drivers toward the end of the season to try to make the boys run away in desperation without collecting their season's wages.

Various mission societies tried to help the boy hoggees—who needed all the help they could get. One missionary, Deacon Eaton, served for five years on the Erie and left a book about his experiences. He estimated that out of the total force of 25,000 people working on the canal in 1845, nearly 5,000 were young boy drivers, many of them orphans. He tells of one captain who threw a sick boy out in a swamp where he was found the next day lying on logs onto which he had dragged himself; the boy died less than two hours after he was found.

The deacon writes of another boy who was so ill that he fell off his horse and knocked himself unconcious, badly gashing his head. The unfeeling captain had the boy dragged aside and made the other hoggee take over and drive on. Someone asked a near-by locktender if he would help but he replied, "No, I wish he was dead. He is the wickedest boy on the canal." So the lad lay senseless in the hot sun for several hours. At last a man came along who took pity on the boy, carried him to his home, and called a doctor. Days passed before the lad recovered his senses. When he was well enough he was asked if he really was the wickedest boy on the Erie Canal as the locktender had said. He answered that he supposed he must be because after five years of being treated like a slave and cheated out of his pay, he had learned to lie, steal, and get drunk. The story, according to Deacon Eaton, had a happy ending. The boy recovered, got a job with a good captain, and five years later was a captain himself.

For captains, boys, and horses, the Erie was easy navigating compared to many canals—especially those that entered streams for portions of their courses. These added currents, sand-bars, and other such hazards to the ordinary problems of canalboat hand-ling. Yet the best-known song about the terrors of shipwreck along the towpath, is a ballad about "The E-RI-E." The first, third, and sixth verses will give an idea of some of the fearful experiences that could beset a sailor on the canal:

We were forty miles from Albany,
    Forget it I never shall;
What a terrible storm we had that night
    On the E-ri-e Canal.

CHORUS:
    O-o-oh, the E-ri-e was a-rising,
    The gin was a-getting low,
    And I scarcely think
    We'll get a drink
    Till we get to Buffalo-o-o,
    Till we get to Buffalo.

The hoggee, riding one of three horses at left, must soon get ready to relax his line and let the horses of the oncoming barge go past.

Our captain he came up on deck
   With his spyglass in his hand,
And the fog it was so tarnal thick
   That he couldn't spy the land.
The winds began to whistle
   And the waves began to roll,
And we had to reef our royals
   On the raging canawl.

The perils of a raging storm on a channel four feet deep and forty feet wide were, of course, quite exaggerated. Even where the depth was seven feet and the width increased, the danger of shipwreck was slight. But there was a grain of truth in the joking, for a great many boats had accidents on the Erie—and on other canals throughout the country.

Another important member of the canal force was the towpath walker, or pathmaster. His job was to patrol a ten-mile section of towpath and berm each day. The principal tool of his profession was a sack full of manure and hay. If he found a small leak, he stuffed the mixture inside it and sealed it by stamping it down. If the leak was beyond such simple repair measures, he called for help in a hurry. Muskrat burrows in the banks were a common cause of leaks and the animals were thoroughly hated by canawlers. A small leak could grow so quickly that whole sections of bank would suddenly crumble away. Then

Two barges are high and dry on a section of a canal in Pennsylvania that has been filled with silt from the flooding of the adjacent river.

A portrait of boisterous nightlife along the Erie, this brightly lit Syracuse square shows strollers and vendors beside the canal.

the water would drain out of the canal leaving boats mudlarked on the bottom.

Slim and speedy repair boats pulled by fast horses were stationed at intervals along the canal, ready to answer emergency calls at a moment's notice. On board were ropes, shovels, timbers, hay, axes, and everything else needed to repair a breach. They foamed along at ten miles an hour, and were appropriately called "hurry-up boats." When there was a break in the canal, everyone—boatcrews and locktenders alike—worked night and day to get it repaired, because there was no way to detour around a section without any water in it.

A locktender had to have a handy pair of fists to settle arguments, and a knack of getting along without sleep. There were times when boats would be waiting to go through the locks twenty four hours a day. Although he had a few assistants, the locktender had to be on hand most

127

One of New York's several villages that the Erie made into cities,
Buffalo grew from a handful of houses in 1795 to the busy shipping
center above soon after the canal opened. By 1832, the population
was 15,000; by 1853, Buffalo had become the sprawling city below.

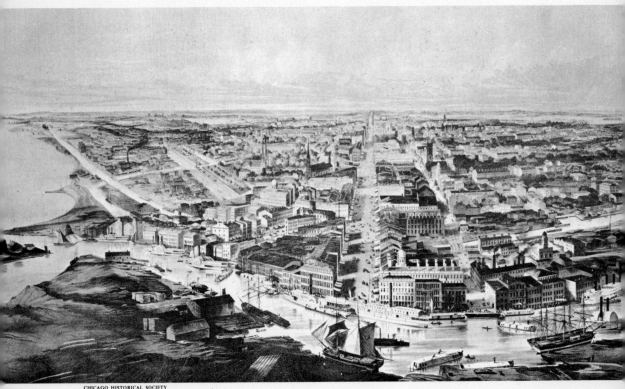

of the time himself to supervise the seemingly endless openings and closings of the lock gates.

Stretched out along the canal were the shops that catered to the canal-boats. A captain could tie up in front of them and buy a firkin of salt mackerel or a bushel of oats, have a horse shod or get a gallon of whiskey, and pick up the latest news at the same time. There was a grocery store, and sometimes two, at every lock—and in those days they sold a great many things besides food. Almost all of them carried liquor, which being very cheap was drunk in great quantities.

The Erie Canal itself affected the people and territory of western New York State like strong tonic. Before the Erie was dug, only the Mohawk Valley end of the route was populated, and some of that pretty thinly. From Rome west to Buffalo there was only wilderness except for rare scattered clearings where a few cabins clustered together and pretended to be a village. But how they grew!

Colonel William L. Stone, who made a trip on the Erie in 1829, had been over the same course nine years earlier when the canal was being built. His remarks about Syracuse were typical of his amazement at the changes he found: "I looked about upon the village as I stept upon shore with still more astonishment than at Utica. 'Another enchanted city,' I exclaimed, as I glanced upwards and around upon splendid hotels and rows of massive buildings in all di-rections—crowded, too, with people all full of life and activity! Nine years before, I had passed a day here among some five or six scattered tenements . . . the whole being surrounded by a desolate, poverty-stricken, woody country, enough to make an owl weep to fly over it."

The colonel's remarks about Syracuse being an enchanted city should be taken with a grain of salt because it was still a new and raw community. And it was completely without trees. Colonel Stone observed that the people in all the new villages seemed to look on the forest as their enemy, and they cut down every single tree. But the colonel noted that after a year or two the settler, detesting his ugly, treeless village, "now hates worse the clearings, and so all are busy planting saplings which will take a hundred years to equal their predecessors."

Syracuse was a city of salt. Springs of briny water came out of the earth, and even before the canal was built salt was already being extracted from them. But the saltmakers had a hard time getting their product to market, and the industry remained small. Then Clinton's Ditch came, and Syracuse began to ship its salt everywhere —by the hundreds and thousands of tons. Dozens of saltworks sprang up, and the city became the greatest salt producer in the nation.

Other canal communities also developed their own industries. Stump Town became so prosperous by shipping its fine buckskin gloves to market

on the canal, that the town changed its name to Gloversville. Amsterdam put in a rug loom and did so well that in time it became a national center for carpet making. The residents of Little Falls switched from their old boat-hauling service to manufacturing. A gazeteer for 1840 listed the local industries as four iron furnaces, three paper mills, a woolen mill, two plaster factories, a machine shop, a fulling mill for cloth, a trip hammer, a brewery, a distillery, and a window sash factory. It was the Mohawk River, rushing over the falls, that provided power for all this industry. But water power alone would not have brought in factories. Without the Erie Canal to transport its products, Little Falls would have remained no more than a village by a beautiful waterfall.

Rochester was a great boom town on the western half of the Erie. Here the canal crossed the deep and rugged Genesee River which tumbled over rapids and waterfalls, ready to power new industry. The swiftness of Rochester's growth was fantastic. The clearing crews hurriedly felled trees to make more room for buildings, but had no time to pull stumps. So while the town boomed, the stumps left in the streets began to sprout. It was said that when the population reached 13,000, the streets were still so filled with brush that a stagecoach took an hour to thread its two-mile course through town.

But no one worried about a little brush in the streets with new industries springing up every day. The racing waters of the Genesee gave

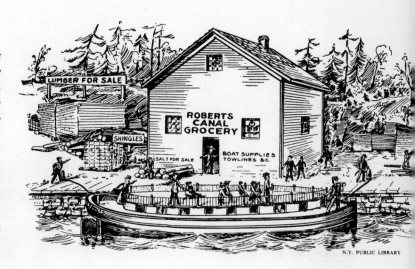

Among the many buildings that owe their life to the Erie were canalside inns and grocery stores. The Canal House (left) dominates a heavily traveled part of the Erie. At right is a store that not only supplied food and hardware but also served as a packet stop. The Frances, *in front, is casting off. A man unties her bow line; another blows the departure horn.*

power to one waterwheel after another as the new factories started up. Stores began selling goods even before their roofs were finished. Speculators were buying up building lots in the uncleared forest and quickly selling them for huge profits. Eleven flour mills made Rochester one of the greatest milling centers in the world. Her millstones turned night and day, grinding out flour so endlessly that warehouse space ran out, and the barrels of flour had to be piled in the open. Rochester also became the center for canalboat construction. Hundreds of vessels were turned out in her boatyards; and by 1835, nearly half the boats on the Erie were owned or controlled by Rochester interests.

The canals in other states also had their boom cities. But towns near waterways open only a short time often faded away again to tiny hamlets or a few moss-grown cellar holes. Cincinnati, Cleveland, Toledo, and Dayton all boomed from villages to great cities because of the prosperity the long-running Ohio canal system brought to them.

Of all the many events that touched the Erie communities, the most tragic was a devastating epidemic of cholera. The outbreak of the highly-contagious disease started in Asia. Spread by infected travelers, it reached out across Europe and was then carried to Canada by three or four boatloads of Irish immigrants. The epidemic struck Montreal and Quebec in the spring of 1832. Within eleven days it had killed over three thousand people. Before the summer was out, some 600

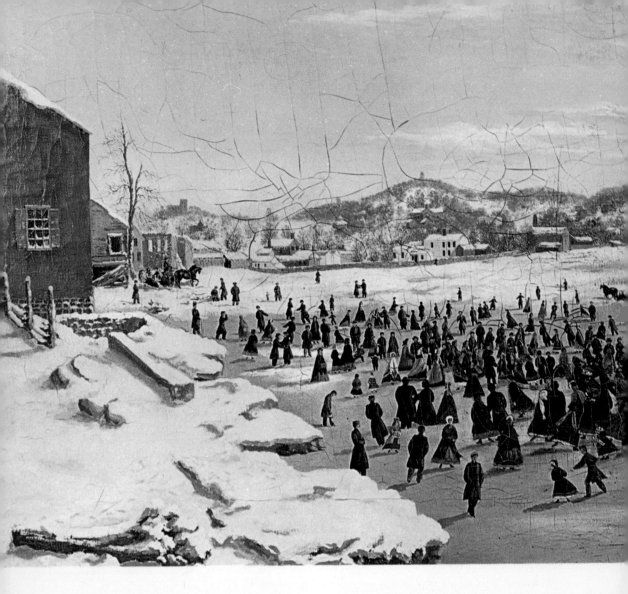

more lay dead in each Canadian city.

More travelers carried the cholera along the St. Lawrence River and down the Champlain Canal to Albany, as well as from New York City up the Hudson. Albany had its first death in mid-June. From there, the disease raced down the Erie Canal carried by victims who probably felt fine when they started, but sickened suddenly—and often died—on the way.

Doctors at that time did not know what caused cholera. At first they gave out comforting statements saying that the illness was not contagious and that its victims were almost always from the lowest level of society—the shiftless, the ignorant, the drunkards. Just shun strong drink, the medical men said, and close your windows tight at night to keep out the dangerous night air, and all would be well. But when the rich as well as the poor, and the hard-working as well as the shiftless were struck down, the doctors had to admit that

This winter scene at Rochester, the city which benefited most from the canal, shows some of the prosperous and growing population skating on the frozen waters of the Genesee River. The Genesee's swift water supplied power for Rochester's factories—the Erie's water carried their produce east and west. The date of this cracked painting is 1863, by which time the railroad as well as the canal had come to Rochester (note the railcars in the background at right).

they could give no definite answers.

One fairly accurate theory held that the cholera came from tainted soil and reached humans through fruits and vegetables they ate. But then the Utica newspaper quoted an unnamed authority who proposed that people wear wooden shoes so that they would not absorb the cholera influence through their feet. The most prevalent theory, however, was that the disease was spread by some sort of mysterious vapor in the air. One story (which is still circulating today) has it that the citizens of Syracuse tested out the vapor theory by tying a large beef roast to a church steeple. When it was brought down an hour later, it was completely rotten— or so it was claimed. But many people suspected funny business and believed the meat must have been pretty mellow when it was put up. Some other canal towns, nevertheless, took to putting large pieces of meat on poles in the hope that it would soak up the cholera vapor in the air.

Nothing seemed to slow the spread of the disease. Few places along the canal were spared. People who could, fled the towns to high country. Hoping to avoid contact with the dread disease, farmers refused to transport produce to cities and towns. Stores closed and food became scarce. Soon, people were actually dying in the streets. The air along the canal was murky from burning barrels of tar which many communities kept going night and day in the belief that the heavy black smoke rid the air of cholera. Lime was believed to have the same power, and vats of it bubbled and fumed on street corners.

There were very few hospitals anywhere in 1832. Emergency ones were set up in an abandoned warehouse in Utica, a canalside barrel factory in Rochester, the poorhouse in Albany, and similar large buildings in other towns. The sick were so numerous that they crowded every inch of space. They were laid on beds of straw on the floor in suffocating, evil-smelling wards where the windows were tightly closed against the night air with its supposed poisons.

Very soon traffic on the canal had almost completely stopped. Some communities refused to allow boats to enter their borders. Others rushed the boats through, not even allowing passengers who had reached their destination to get off.

The epidemic was not limited to the Erie Canal. It quickly spread to Boston and other ports about the same time it hit Canada. It was carried west and south by infected passengers who changed from canalboats to ships on the Great Lakes. From there the cholera raced along the Ohio canal system and down the Mississippi River and its branches. It missed few places where men went: New Orleans lost 10,000 that summer.

With the coming of autumn, however, the disease seemed to have run the course of susceptible people. Slowly, things began to return to normal. Captains waited impatiently at locks, wanting to make up at least some of the season's lost time before freeze-up. Hoggees shivered in the early morning chill as leaves dropped from the trees and rustled on the towpath. But the afternoon sun was still warm, and soon small boys fished once again from the berm, and housewives gossiped from their back porches. It seemed wiser to everyone to look toward the future than back on the months of terror.

Canal life had its joys as well as its sorrows. If there were epidemics, there were also floating circuses. The Spalding and Rogers Circus, advertised in the poster at right, played to crowded and enthusiastic audiences up and down the Wabash and Erie Canal. Sig Sawtelle's circus boat, tied up for the winter at Syracuse (below), was busy in other seasons bringing acrobatic and animal acts to Erie dwellers. The mob scene beside the canal in this photograph is the Syracuse Farmers' Market, a regular outdoor gathering of buyers and sellers.

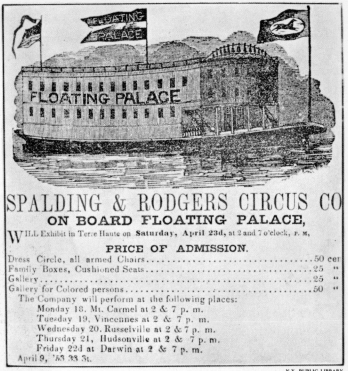

FLOATING PALACE

FLOATING PALACE

SPALDING & RODGERS CIRCUS CO

ON BOARD FLOATING PALACE,

WILL Exhibit in Terre Haute on **Saturday, April 23d**, at 2 and 7 o'clock, P. M,

PRICE OF ADMISSION.

Dress Circle, all armed Chairs......................................50 cer
Family Boxes, Cushioned Seats.....................................25 "
Gallery..25 "
Gallery for Colored persons.......................................50 "

The Company will perform at the following places:
Monday 18. Mt. Carmel at 2 & 7 p. m.
Tuesday 19, Vincennes at 2 & 7 p. m.
Wednesday 20. Russelville at 2 & 7 p. m.
Thursday 21, Hudsonville at 2 & 7 p. m.
Friday 22d at Darwin at 2 & 7 p. m.
April 9, '53 33 3t.

7 END OF AN ERA

The heyday of the canals lasted no more than thirty years. The era spans no definite period of time but runs from the digging of the Erie Canal to the middle of the century, approximately 1820–1850. By the end of that time hardly a shovel was being turned on new waterways. Many of the existing ones soon fell into neglect and were abandoned. (If tombstones had later been placed beside the miles of empty ditches and rotting locks, their epitaphs would read: Here lies a great canal, done to death by the steam locomotive.)

Yet, it was a canal which brought the first locomotive to this country. The Delaware and Hudson Canal, which ran more than a hundred miles from Honesdale, Pennsylvania, to Rondout, New York, operated packets and freight boats like most waterways; but its main business was hauling anthracite coal. To get the coal from the mines to the canal at Honesdale, a sixteen-mile railway was built in 1826. The cars ran along an inclined plane and coasted to their destination. Not long afterward, the company learned that English mines had been successfully using steam locomotives on mine railways since 1811.

The Chesapeake and Ohio Canal flows beside the Potomac River in this 1860 primitive view of Harpers Ferry. And beside the canal runs the steam railroad—soon to dominate American transportation.

So they decided to try steam themselves and sent to England for a locomotive. The shiny new Stourbridge Lion made only one run. The engine itself proved successful; but the roadbed on which the tracks were laid had not been built to sustain such a heavy load for repeated runs. Sadly, the company retired the Lion to a shed and it never moved under its own power again.

Other locomotives, however, were soon in full-time operation. On Christmas Day in 1830, an American-made locomotive began running on a railway in Charleston, South Carolina. Unfortunately it blew up six months later fatally injuring the fireman, who was sitting on the safety valve to stop the hiss of escaping steam which annoyed him.

Peter Cooper, a wealthy manufacturer from New York, built his tiny locomotive, the Tom Thumb, for the Baltimore and Ohio Railroad. He set up a contest between his engine and a well-known race horse to prove that steam could do better than horses. The Tom Thumb lost when a leak in the boiler lowered the pressure and seriously cut down its speed. But the test still managed to demonstrate the increased possibilities of steam. Before long, locomotives were replacing horses all along the Baltimore and Ohio Railroad.

About the same time, another railway company, the Mohawk and Hudson, went into competition with the Erie Canal. It ran seventeen miles from Albany to Schenectady, and tried to win away those canalboat passengers who wanted to avoid the tedious journey through the many locks between the two towns. But the railroad gave its passengers a terrifying ride. They were seated on open flatcars which raced along at twenty miles an hour. They were choked and blinded by thick, sooty smoke, and constantly menaced by showers of fiery sparks. It was even doubtful that the train would be able to stop at the end of the trip, and track had to be laid up ramps to hold the train if the brakes failed. At the time, this steam-powered joy ride offered little serious competition to the Erie. In later years, however, the Mohawk and Hudson became one of the links in the New York Central Railroad system which, in turn, became one of America's big freight and passenger carriers—and seriously cut into the Erie's business.

During the 1830's other railroads appeared here and there, as far west as Michigan and Indiana. But the canals were still the darlings of the nation, for railways were only in the experimental stage. The men who were pinning their hopes on cars that ran on rails were not even sure how they were going to propel them. Some companies, like the early Baltimore and Ohio, depended on horses. Others experimented with putting the horse on a flatcar where he walked on a treadmill geared to the wheels. Even sails were tried, and they worked

A boatman gestures angrily and a tow horse rears in fear as a loco-motive runs noisily along a bank of the Chesapeake and Ohio Canal.

fine as long as there was a wind—and it was blowing from the right direction. But it was the steam locomotive which eventually replaced all of these early methods.

Even while the canals were booming, the railroads were busy laying a few miles of track here, a few more miles there. The little locomotives were getting better, and they were less likely to break down or blow up. They were now able to haul more freight and passengers even though they still had to stop every six miles to take on wood and water to fuel the engine. Very soon the railroads

A lock on an abandoned canal (above) crumbles into decay—a disappearing relic of an era that ended almost as suddenly as it began.

began to catch the fancy of America. Many of the people who had clamored for the canals now found them old-fashioned; they could be satisfied with nothing less than a railroad.

A great debate went on between those who wanted the speed the railroads could provide, and those who supported the dependability of the canals. It was against God's law, said the canal people, for men to go roaring across the land at fifteen or even twenty miles an hour. Then, there were the doctors who doubted that the human body could stand such speeds without suffering serious mental and physical ailments, including possible boiling of the blood. The railroad supporters pooh-poohed all of these arguments except the last. But most Americans, because of the great size of their country, were always in a hurry to get places, and rather liked the idea of all that speed.

As the years passed, a strange thing happened. People not only lost interest in the waterways with the coming of the railroads, but many of them developed an actual hate for the canals they had once welcomed with fireworks and cheers. By the middle of the century, men were gathering in protest meetings which often ended in raiding parties. They damaged locks, burned aqueducts, and cut holes into canal banks to let the escaping water rip out whole sections of channel.

It is difficult to understand such malicious destruction, especially when hundreds of thousands of people still

140

depended on the canals for their livelihood. Part of it was due to the huge canal debt. Those same people who had pushed for the digging of so many canals, now began to lay the blame for the debt on the waterways, instead of on themselves. Another part of the anti-canal fervor was the result of ignorance and superstition. The idea had spread that the canals and their reservoirs carried agues and fevers.

Indiana's great Wabash and Erie Canal, which had cost so much in human life and heartache and money —and yet had repaid everything by bringing the state out of the wilderness—was one of many victims of this senseless vandalism. In 1855, when the last mile of the long waterway was not yet quite done, a mob of men with disguised faces descended on the canal. They set an aqueduct afire, and blew up the dam of the great Birch Creek Reservoir, destroying the water supply for a long section of canal. It was repaired at great expense after several months' work; but boats had hardly begun to move in the channel before the reservoir was wrecked again. It was repaired once more, and the people to whom the canal still meant a great deal rejoiced. But by then the canal era was ending. Within four short years, flood damage, rotting aqueducts, and general neglect put more sections of the Indiana canals permanently out of service more effectively than any of the canal-hating mobs had been able to do.

Many canals suffered from neglect.

Two mules (above), perhaps the last tow team in the country, pull this tourist boat on a remnant of the C & O Canal in Washington.

As sections fell into disrepair they were abandoned, for people were convinced that expenditures for repairs were hardly worth making. Few, if any, of the man-made waterways had been able to recoup their building costs, or to set aside reserve funds for even emergency repairs in case of severe damage from floods or other unforeseen disasters.

In a few scattered areas, some sec-

141

Spewing black smoke, a locomotive with passenger cars hurries by a freight barge on the berm of a Pennsylvania canal. The train still appears to be a curiosity to onlookers in this 1850 view.

tions continued to operate for years after the canal as a whole had ceased to carry traffic. Mule teams leisurely towed weather-beaten old boats down the remaining lengths of channel passing through moss-grown locks, to serve villages still far from any railroad. Finally, even these bits of canal were gone, too. The Pennsylvania Grand Canal, with its Portage Railroad and other expensive complications did not last long after the canal

era began to fade. But portions of the Pennsylvania branch canals saw mules and horses on their towpaths until well after the First World War. It was no longer an exciting waterway crammed with packets and lineboats moving night and day. There were just a few ancient barges with crotchety old captains, hauling cargoes no more romantic than a load of coal. Nevertheless they were canalboats, and they were among the last. Once

142

these battered old barges ceased running along the canal, no new boats would come along to replace them.

The Chesapeake and Ohio Canal along the Potomac never got across the mountains as its backers planned, and it never made much money, but it had a longer life than most. More than once it was badly damaged by floods and looked as though it would have to be abandoned, but each time its backers managed to make the needed repairs. Finally though, a flood in 1924 washed out great parts of it and there was just not enough business to make more repairs worthwhile.

A small section of the Chesapeake and Ohio, however, is still operating; it is one of the last towpath canals in the country. The United States Government acquired the weed-grown waterway, repaired a part of it near Washington, and put a canalboat on it. Today, anyone who goes to the nation's capital can ride on a canalboat pulled by a team of mules treading a towpath in Georgetown.

Even though the hoggee and his team have long since made their last trip and the towpaths themselves have disappeared, a few canals are still in use—with their faces greatly changed. Any boats that run along them now are pushed by tugboats, not pulled on towlines. But these canals are a pitifully small patch on the thousands of miles of waterway that once bustled with activity.

And what of the champion of them all? The great Erie Canal continued to make money while all the others were going into debt; it was always able to repair flood damage and the wear and tear of hard use. For a very long time the railroads could offer no serious competition because the Erie still lay in the most convenient passage through the mountains. In the early part of 1825, half a year before it was completely opened, the canal commissioners reported that the Erie was already too small. They suggested that the locks be doubled, and even hinted that a parallel canal should be built in the eastern section.

The work crews got busy in 1836. In some places two sets of locks were built—all were extended from ninety to one hundred and eighteen feet. The channel, which had generally been forty feet wide and four feet deep, was made seventy feet by seven feet. Many sections of the channel were straightened and relocated, reducing the Albany-Buffalo distance by thirteen miles. Many of the locks were made higher, eliminating several of the original eighty-three.

The first enlargement was completed in 1862. By then the canal era was well past, and many waterways in other states had already returned to wilderness. But the Erie showed no sign of fading. After its enlargement, it could carry boats of up to 250 tons, yet it was still too small: In 1868 the canal carried over three million tons of freight. During this period, and even into the 1880's, it was said that a person standing on a

BOTH: MORAN TOWING & TRANSPORTATION COMPANY

Modern-day scenes on the New York State Barge Canal show (above) a crewman relaxing, and (below) a tugboat pushing a barge along the wider and deeper waterway that replaced the old Erie.

bridge could often see two long lines of boats in either direction as far as his eye could reach, and at night the string of headlamps looked like a torchlight parade.

By 1860 the railroads had grown so strong that they held tremendous political power in New York State, and lobbied to stop canal operations. Some railroads campaigned for the draining of the Erie so that railroad tracks could be laid on its bed. But the Erie belonged to the people of the state, and its friends were able to ward off attacks on it. The packet boats had long since disappeared because they could not possibly compete with the faster passenger trains. But for carrying heavy freight in cases where speed was of no importance, the Erie had broader shoulders than the railroad.

In 1882 all tolls were abolished. By that time the Erie had paid its original cost many times over. Even De Witt Clinton, for all his faith in the Ditch, could never have imagined that its tolls would clear forty-two million dollars. But after the turn of the century, towpath power came to an end for the Erie, too, although the waterway itself still continues a highly useful life.

Beginning in 1903, the Erie Canal and its two main branches—the Champlain Canal, and the Oswego Canal which connected the Erie with Lake Ontario—were cut deeper and widened, and much larger locks with higher lifts were installed. This chain

of waterways, completed in 1918, is known as the New York State Barge Canal System. Including the stretch along the Hudson River, the Barge Canal runs some 800 miles. Much of the old Erie Canal was relocated. It has boldly tamed the once-turbulent Mohawk River with a series of dams, turning it into just another placid length of canal. Huge barges, almost 300 feet long and pushed by diesel-powered boats, now move on a waterway where packet boats once paid fines for speeding faster than four miles an hour.

In some spots the enlarged Erie and the old Erie still use the same course; but on most of the new route, one or both of the later canals have been shifted anywhere from a few feet to a number of miles from the former course. One can still find traces of the overgrown channels and sometimes even a lock—often within easy hearing distance of the whistle of a tugboat pushing barges of gasoline, steel beams, or grain on the modern canal.

Though the Barge Canal is still a workaday route, the color of the early years is no longer there. The canalside grocery stores have gone, and there is no sound of a fiddle coming from a locktender's shack on a rainy night; those things went out with the old Erie. One must imagine them as they were when the hoggee drove his team down the towpath, and the steersman shouted, "Low bridge, everybody down!"

OVERLEAF: *The Mohawk Valley today is still a major corridor to the West. Running through it are three routes, each favored by different eras: the Mohawk River, the Erie Canal, and a superhighway.*

PHOTO BY LAURENCE LOWRY; COURTESY *Holiday*, © 1957, CURTIS PUBLISHING COMPANY

COLDEN, *Memoir*, 1825

The invitation to New York's ball celebrating the opening of the Erie bore this design.

AMERICAN HERITAGE PUBLISHING CO., INC.

PRESIDENT JAMES PARTON

EDITORIAL DIRECTOR JOSEPH J. THORNDIKE, JR.

EDITOR, BOOK DIVISION RICHARD M. KETCHUM

ART DIRECTOR IRWIN GLUSKER

AMERICAN HERITAGE JUNIOR LIBRARY

MANAGING EDITOR RUSSELL BOURNE

ART DIRECTOR ELEANOR A. DYE

ASSOCIATE EDITOR WADE GREENE

CHIEF PICTURE RESEARCHER JULIA POTTS GREHAN

PICTURE RESEARCHER MARY LEVERTY

COPY EDITOR BARBARA FISHER SHOR

EDITORIAL ASSISTANT NANCY SIMON

ACKNOWLEDGMENTS

The Editors are deeply grateful to Mr. Richard N. Wright, President of the Onondaga Historical Association and Secretary-Treasurer of the Canal Society of New York State, for his guidance and advice on the manuscript as well as on pictorial material and sources. They would also like to express their appreciation to Mr. Frank B. Thomson, Director of the Canal Museum in Syracuse, for his generous assistance. In addition, they wish to thank the following individuals and organizations for their assistance and for making available pictorial material in their collections.

Albany Institute of History—Norman S. Rice
Arnold H. Barben, Seneca Falls, New York
Buffalo and Erie County Historical Society—Ivan E. Whitney
C & O Canal National Monument, Hagerstown, Md.—Edwin M. Dale
Dr. David Ennis, Lyons, New York
Fort Stanwix Museum, Rome, New York —Gilbert Hagerty
Albert E. Gayer, Schenectady, New York
Robert H. Glenn, Albany, New York
Robert E. Hager, Syracuse, New York
Indiana Historical Society—Caroline Dunn
Museum of Science and Industry, Chicago—Mary S. Jacobsohn, Bob Kotas
New York State Education Department —Eugene F. Kramer
New York State Historical Association— Louis C. Jones
New York State Library—Donald C. Anthony, Peter J. Paulson
Pennsylvania Historical and Museum Commission—S. K. Stevens, William N. Richards
Rochester Memorial Art Gallery—Isabel C. Herdle
Schenectady City History Center—J. W. Joyce
Shelburne Museum, Vermont—Bradley Smith, Sterling D. Emerson

The painting on pages 14–15, from the Metropolitan Museum of Art, is the gift of Mrs. George E. Schanck in memory of Arthur Hoppock Hearn, 1913. The print on page 27, also from the Metropolitan, is in the Edward W. C. Arnold Collection.

FOR FURTHER READING

Adams, Samuel Hopkins, *Grandfather Stories*. New York, Random House, Inc., 1955.

Caruso, John Anthony, *The Great Lakes Frontier*. Indianapolis, The Bobbs-Merrill Company, 1961.

Dunbar, Seymour, *A History of Travel in America*. New York, Tudor Publishing Company, 1937.

Edmonds, Walter Dumaux, *Erie Water*. Boston, Little, Brown & Company, 1933.

Ellis, David, *et. al., A Short History of New York State*. Ithaca, Cornell University Press, 1957.

Goodrich, Carter, Ed., *Canals and American Economic Development*. New York, Columbia University Press, 1961.

Hansen, Marcus Lee, *The Immigrant in American History*. Cambridge, Harvard University Press, 1940.

Harlow, Alvin F., *Old Towpaths*. New York, Appleton, 1926.

Holbrook, Stewart H., *The Yankee Exodus*. New York, The Macmillan Company, 1950.

Payne, Robert, *The Canal Builders*. New York, The Macmillan Company, 1959.

Riegel, Robert E., *America Moves West*. New York, Henry Holt & Company, Inc., 1956.

Thompson, Harold W., *Body, Boots & Britches*. Philadelphia, J. B. Lippincott Company, 1939.

Waggoner, Madeline Sadler, *The Long Haul West*. New York, G. P. Putnam's Sons, 1958.

Wyld, Lionel D., *Low Bridge!* Syracuse, Syracuse University Press, 1962.

SHELBURNE MUSEUM, VERMONT

Canals were a popular subject for American artists through the nineteenth century. This Erie scene was a design for wallpaper.

INDEX

Bold face indicates pages
on which illustrations appear

A